PLANTS & GARDENS

BROOKLYN BOTANIC GARDEN RECORD

ELVIN McDONALD

THE
WINTER GARDEN

1991

Brooklyn Botanic Garden

STAFF FOR THIS EDITION:

ERICA GLASENER, GUEST EDITOR

BARBARA B. PESCH, DIRECTOR OF PUBLICATIONS

JANET MARINELLI, ASSOCIATE EDITOR

AND THE EDITORIAL COMMITTEE OF THE BROOKLYN BOTANIC GARDEN

BEKKA LINDSTROM, ART DIRECTOR

JUDITH D. ZUK, PRESIDENT, BROOKLYN BOTANIC GARDEN

ELIZABETH SCHOLTZ, DIRECTOR EMERITUS, BROOKLYN BOTANIC GARDEN

STEPHEN K-M. TIM, VICE PRESIDENT, SCIENCE & PUBLICATIONS

COVER: *IRIS RETICULATA*

PHOTOGRAPH BY DEREK FELL

Plants & Gardens, Brooklyn Botanic Garden Record (ISSN 0362-5850) is published quarterly at 1000 Washington Ave., Brooklyn, N.Y. 11225, by the **Brooklyn Botanic Garden, Inc.** Second-class-postage paid at Brooklyn, N.Y., and at additional mailing offices. Subscription included in Botanic Garden membership dues ($25.00) per year).

ISBN # 0-945352-69-7

PLANTS & GARDENS

BROOKLYN BOTANIC GARDEN RECORD

Ref

THE WINTER GARDEN

V O L . 4 7 , N O . 4 , W I N T E R 1 9 9 1

HANDBOOK #129

The Osborne Section at the Brooklyn Botanic Garden
with a frosting of ice and snow.

FOREWORD

Winter has its pleasures — the crunch of snow underfoot, the occasional glazing of ice on leaves and branches, the heady bouquet of a hot toddy. For most gardeners, winter is a time to retire before a crackling fire and make do with the promise of nursery catalogs and the return of spring.

But with a bit of attention, the winter garden can be a place of wonder. To quote Elizabeth Lawrence from her book *Gardens in Winter*, "To be pleasant in winter a garden needs more than trees and shrubs and a green carpet. It must have brick and stone to catch and hold the warmth of the sun, a wall or hedge against the north, and dry pavement underfoot. There may be flowers, and even a momentary splendor when the mume [Japanese flowering apricot] reaches perfection against the pale blue of a January sky, but in winter more than any other season, plants need the support of good design and a well ordered pattern."

When designing the winter garden, think about the view from the inside looking out, including the vistas beyond the boundaries of your garden. Choose carefully those plants not only around windows but also doorways and well travelled walks. Evergreens are effective but should not be overdone. In *The Garden in Winter*, Rosemary Verey recommends that you have a corner in your winter garden, "however small, where you can be sure of finding those special flowers that brave the weather, those leaves that keep their colour and those berries that hang on through the winter days. And it should be tucked away so that you have a positive inducement to walk out of the house...."

Ms. Verey also writes that "Winter colour is nature's most sophisticated palette — a range dominated by subtle tones, sombre contrasts and striking highlights. For the winter gardener, the challenge is to enhance and build upon this mellow array."

May this collection of articles inspire you to plant for winter interest or to add a winter corner to your existing garden where you can enjoy the special fragrances, colors and textures of this often overlooked season.

ERICA GLASENER
GUEST EDITOR

5

THE BARE ESSENTIALS

BY GARY L. KOLLER

For most people winter is a time to plan the spring and summer garden. During autumn when frosts arrive and the lush display of summer is just a memory, many gardens become drab and lifeless. With careful planning, the winter garden can have its own visual pleasures.

What can you do to enhance the visual pleasures of your winter garden? Once flowers fade and leaves fall the landscape is distilled to its bare essentials. Consequently, my first suggestion is that you take a hard look at your garden's bones — its underlying design, walls, hedges, pathways and outstanding plant specimens and other focal points. Take walks along neighborhood streets and through parks and natural areas in search of ideas, or

GARY L. KOLLER *is Assistant Director of Horticulture at the Arnold Arboretum, a lecturer in landscape architecture at Harvard University's Graduate School of Design and co-author of* Street Trees for Home and Municipal Landscapes.

visit gardens at this time of year when their bones are most evident. Garden clubs and plant societies rarely take winter garden tours, but much could be gained if they did.

A good place to start improving the winter garden is the view from a favorite window. During the summer we tend not to look outward to the landscape as frequently or for as long as we do in winter. Or, you can convert a summer scene which you largely ignore to a winter picture whose beauty and form lasts for weeks or months. But you don't have to stop there. It is possible to improve design throughout the garden to make it more appealing in winter.

Walls and Garden Structures

In winter garden walls, fences, pergolas, latticework and other structures are revealed in all their splendor — or squalor, as the case may be. Stone walls, for example, which are largely hidden in summer, become dominant visual features once the foliage is cut back. Walls are especially beautiful with a frosting of ice and snow, as the remains of herbaceous plants glisten and cast shadows.

In summer, garden structures are often simply props for plants. But in winter, they themselves become the focal points. If the design of your garden structures leaves much to be desired, improving them can make a dramatic difference in the winter garden. Sometimes all that is needed is a bit of tender loving care; a new coat of paint can work wonders.

Many homes and associated structures have large, blank walls — ideal candidates for imaginative horticultural treatment. Consider taking a stiffly upright tree with a distinctive branching structure, such as the fastigiate goldenrain tree (*Koelreuteria paniculata* 'Fastigiata') or the columnar sugar maple (*Acer saccharum* 'Columnare') and planting it as an accent piece far enough away from the wall to cast shadows on it. Or consider espaliering a winter-blooming shrub like witch-hazel against a wall or undistinguished fence.

Organization of Space

In winter how you organize space in the garden is most apparent. The mix of deciduous and evergreen plants may lack visual unity, spatial organization or flow. Have you ever visited a garden which works wonderfully during summer but fails spatially as a wintertime composition? Many gardeners assume that evergreens are the cure-all for the winter garden, the more the better. But I have been in several gardens which were evergreen or largely evergreen and look somber, cold and drab in the wintertime. What looks more pitiful than a rhododendron with its leaves curled? Also, a preponderance of evergreens will mean that there is little change between the summer and winter garden. I find it exciting to

anticipate the change which results from having a judicious mix of evergreens, deciduous plants and herbaceous perennials. But as the change unfolds I still want the components to work together at each season.

Observe the unoccupied, or negative, spaces between the buildings, the plantings and other "positive" elements such as walls, fences and garden ornaments. How do the positive elements relate to the negative spaces? Is there a feeling of cohesiveness and design flow? Are all the elements integrated into a spatial image which transcends any one component and becomes a part of the whole?

During the dormant season the absence of foliage on trees and shrubs reveals views obscured in summer. If the view is good, you might enhance it by removing plants, artfully pruning or restructuring the plantings by moving or adding plants.

If winter reveals objectionable views you may also want to group the plantings. Tall, thin plants are useful as visual barriers. One example I recall distinctly was a house which looked out on a beautiful garden. But just beyond a three-story house loomed over the garden. A hedge of 20-foot-tall white pines (*Pinus strobus* 'Fastigiata') was planted at the property edge to enclose the garden and create an open screen which diminished the neighboring house's imposing presence. But keep in mind that any changes you make to enhance the winter garden should not detract from the summer garden.

Plant Form

Many of the techniques for good composition used in the summer garden are of equal use in the winter garden, such as height, form, texture and color.

Height, form, texture, color and other elements of good composition are as important in the winter garden as in the summer garden.

8

Once flowers fade and leaves fall, a garden is distilled to its bare bones —
walls, hedges, pathways and outstanding plant specimens.
In this Northwest winter garden, red- and yellow-flowering witch-hazels
are framed by clipped box hedges.

As leaves fall each autumn, poor pruning and less-than-scrupulous maintenance become ever more obvious. Foundation and border plantings drop their leaves to expose maimed and brutalized thickets of twigs resulting from inept, inappropriate or uninformed pruning. Even if they haven't been brutalized by poor pruning, existing plants can be made more sculptural and artistic if they are thinned to enhance line and form. Indeed, much of what makes a Japanese garden beautiful is the skillful pruning and the attention lavished on individual plants. Evaluate your existing plants for such opportunities.

Herbaceous plants also create artistic forms in the winter garden. As a student of horticulture, I was told that once frost reigned upon the land you were supposed to rush out and prune things back, tidy up and mulch before winter set in. I have since discovered that many of the herbaceous perennials look just as lovely in the winter landscape as in the summer as their foliage turns beige, brown, maroon and silver and their interesting seed structures become more apparent. These rich, warm tones relieve the drab grays, dark browns and monotonous greens of the typical winter garden. Now, many of the same plants I used to chop back with abandon remain in place until I find them unattractive. Allowing plants to remain adds bulk, mass and height to the ground plane and keeps the

SELECT PLANTS FOR THE WINTER GARDEN

WEEPING AND CONTORTED

Abies alba 'Pendula'

Acer palmatum 'Viridis'

Acer palmatum 'Waterfall'

Betula pendula 'Gracilis'

Caragana arborescens 'Pendula'

Cedrus atlantica 'Glauca Pendula'

Cercidiphyllum japonicum 'Pendula'

C. magnificum 'Pendulum'

Chamaecyparis nootkatensis 'Pendula'

Corylus avellana 'Contorta'

Fagus sylvatica 'Pendula'

F. sylvatica 'Tortuosa'

Juniperus rigida 'Pendula'

Larix decidua 'Pendula'

L. x eurolepis 'Vaned Directions'

Morus alba 'Pendula'

M. bombycis 'Unryu'

Picea abies 'Inversa'

P. abies 'Pendula'

P. breweriana

P. omorika 'Pendula'

P. pungens 'Pendula'

Pinus strobus 'Pendula'

Prunus subhirtella 'Pendula'

Pseudotsuga menziesii 'Pendula'

Salix alba 'Tristis'

S. matsudana 'Tortuosa'

Sequoiadendron giganteum 'Pendulum'

Sophora japonica 'Pendula'

Styrax japonicus 'Pendula'

Thuja occidentalis 'Pendula'

Ulmus glabra 'Camperdownii'

U. glabra 'Pendula'

FASTIGIATE AND NARROWLY UPRIGHT

Abies alba 'Pyramidalis'

Acer platanoides 'Columnare'

A. platanoides 'Crimson Sentry'

A. rubrum 'Columnare'

A. platanoides 'Erectum'

A. saccharum 'Columnare'

A. saccharum 'Monumentale'

Betula pendula 'Fastigiata'

Calocedrus decurrens (Columnar in northern part of range)

Cedrus atlantica 'Fastigiata'

Chamaecyparis lawsoniana 'Allumii Magnifica'

C. lawsoniana 'Columnaris'

C. lawsoniana 'Fletcheri'

C. nootkatensis 'Green Arrow'

C. thyoides

Cryptomeria japonica

Cupressus sempervirens 'Stricta'

C. sempervirens 'Swane's Golden'

Fagus sylvatica 'Dawyckii'

(F. sylvatica 'Fastigiata')

Ginkgo biloba 'Sentry'

Juniperus chinensis 'Columnaris'

J. chinensis 'Columnaris Glauca'

J. scopulorum 'Skyrocket'

J. scopulorum 'Sparkling Skyrocket'

Koelreuteria paniculata 'Fastigiata'

Malus baccata 'Columnaris'

M. 'Van Eseltine'

Picea omorika

P. orientalis

Pinus strobus 'Fastigiata'

P. sylvestris 'Fastigiata'
P. sylvestris 'Sentinel'
Populus alba 'Pyramidalis'
P. nigra 'Italica'
Prunus sargentii 'Columnaris'
Pyrus calleryana 'Capital'
Quercus robur 'Fastigiata'
Taxodium ascendens
Taxus baccata 'Fastigiata'
Thuja occidentalis 'Hetz Wintergreen'

Colorful Winter Foliage

Abies concolor 'Candicans'
A. koreana 'Aurea'
A. lasiocarpa 'Glauca'
A. pinsapo 'Glauca'
A. procera 'Aurea'
A. procera 'Glauca'
Buxus sempervirens 'Variegata'
Calluna vulgaris (cultivars)
Cedrus atlantica 'Aurea'
C. atlantica 'Glauca'
C. deodara 'Klondike'
Chamaecyparis lawsoniana 'Minima Aurea'
C. lawsoniana 'Pembury Blue'
C. nootkatensis 'Aurea'
C. nootkatensis 'Glauca'
C. nootkatensis 'Variegata'
C. obtusa 'Aurea'
C. obtusa 'Crippsii'
C. obtusa 'Mariesii'
C. obtusa 'Pygmaea Aurescens'
C. obtusa 'Sanderi'
C. obtusa 'Tetragona Aurea'
C. pisifera 'Boulevard'
C. pisifera 'Filifera Aurea'

C. pisifera 'Plumosa Aurea'
C. pisifera 'Snow'
C. pisifera 'Squarrosa'
C. thyoides 'Heatherbun'
Cryptomeria japonica 'Sekkan Sugi'
Cunninghamia lanceolata 'Glauca'
Cupressus glabra 'Blue Ice'
x *Cupressocyparis leylandii* 'Silver Dust'
Daphne x *burkwoodii* 'Carol Mackie'
Erica carnea cultivars
Juniperus chinensis, communis, deppeana, horizontalis, scopulorum (many good color forms)
Leucothoe fontanesiana 'Girard's Rainbow'
Ligustrum japonicum 'Variegatum'
Liriope muscari 'Variegata'
Picea glauca 'Sander's Blue'
P. orientalis 'Skylands'
P. pungens 'Hoopsii'
P. pungens 'Moerheimii'
Pinus densiflora 'Oculus-draconis'
P. mugo 'Aurea'
P. mugo 'Aurea Fastigiata'
P. parviflora 'Glauca'
P. strobus 'Hillside Winter Gold'
P. thunbergiana 'Oculus-draconis'
P. virginiana 'Wate's Golden'
P. wallichiana 'Zebrina'
Platycladus orientalis 'Berckmannii'
Thuja occidentalis 'Golden Globe'
T. occidentalis 'George Peabody'
T. plicata 'Canadian Gold'
Thujopsis dolobrata 'Variegata'
Tsuga canadensis 'Golden Splendor'

Sculpture, statuary and other garden ornaments which are often eclipsed by summer's foliage can become focal points of the winter garden.
The greyhound above sports a bittersweet wreath.

Many homes and associated structures have large, blank surfaces —
ideal candidates for imaginative horticultural treatment.
Here, espaliered red quince perks up a masonry wall in winter.

In winter when branches are bare, plants with interesting shapes, such as *Corylus avellana* 'Contorta', above, are transformed into living sculpture.

Scrutinize the colors and textures of your winter landscape. A striking combination such as the silver-blue foliage of juniper and red crabapples above provides visual excitement.

scene from looking flat and boring. Many plants become star performers as they poke through ice and snow to cast shadows, provide texture and movement and in some cases sounds — such as the rustling of grasses and bamboos. I've found that my sensitivity to the winter garden has changed as I now look forward to the subtle, sophisticated charms waiting to be discovered. The winter garden has taught me to look closer at the diversity of textures and forms and fine gradations of color.

As winter wears on, some of the herbaceous plants get crushed by ice and snow and some fade in color or become tattered. Throughout the winter on mild days, I go out and remove plants which no longer look attractive. This means that there is a constant change of scene. But it

always amazes me how long many plants remain handsome. In some instances, such as the ornamental grasses, I sacrifice the attractive remains of the plant only to make way for early season bulbs. When to finally cut them back is always a close call. I wait until the shoots of the first bulbs barely poke through the soil and then hesitantly remove the grasses. As much as I look forward to the early season bulbs and the return of spring, there is something wistful about removing the remains of last season's foliage — like finishing a good book.

Color and Texture

Scrutinize the colors and textures of your winter landscape to make sure that they provide visual excitement or a sense of place or peacefulness. Do the evergreens afford a pleasing composition of different textures and shades of green? In the summer garden we talk about bold foliage advancing into view and finer textures receding. But we forget that they do this in wintertime as well. As for texture, there are the narrow, fine-textured needles of pines, the bolder, broader foliage of hollies and, in mild-winter areas, the large leaves of the evergreen magnolias.

Many plants have winter foliage in shades of yellow to gold, silver to gray, maroon to plum and beige to warm browns. These colors are often combined with interesting texture, providing the garden designer with many possibilities for the winter landscape. Again, we tend to look at individual plants when we consider color, but if the garden scene is to be successful the colors need to be blended into one harmonious whole.

I happen to admire color in winter twigs. Many books emphasize those plants which are especially dramatic, such as the red-stemmed dogwoods, the stewartias with their exfoliating bark and the white-stemmed brambles. These are all beautiful and have their place in the winter garden — if they are used as elements of the larger composition and don't just draw attention to themselves. Even the more commonly grown garden plants have color, although it is subtler and requires a more trained eye to discern. Some of the plants actually change color over time due to exposure to sunlight or the effects of temperature. The best stem color is generally in full sun. Some plants such as the willows exhibit best color in the dead of winter but anticipate the return of spring by brightening and intensifying in color as the days lengthen and temperatures rise.

Garden Ornaments

Sculpture, statuary, sundials and other garden ornaments which often recede into summer's foliage can become focal points of the garden in winter. Birdbaths and shallow pools where birds drink and splash literally bring the winter garden to life.

Sculpture is often designed to be a center of attraction in both the summer and winter garden. However, an intriguing alternative is to have a piece of sculpture which is largely hidden in the summer become revealed as a focal point in winter. Large herbaceous plants such as *Miscanthus*, *Boltonia* or *Veronicastrum* could serve as the seasonal mask.

Other potential forms of sculpture are the structures and wrappings we use to protect plants from winter wind and cold. In general, we give these little thought, employing the most functional, and often unattractive, materials. However, in Japan, great attention is paid to making these protective structures beautiful. Often they're presented as important design elements in themselves.

Living Sculpture

Living sculpture is still another possibility. An old plant with an interesting shape can be transformed into a focus of the winter garden. I remember a beautiful modern house in Minnesota with many windows looking out on a lake. One window looked out onto a narrow exterior corridor through a French lilac which had been strategically placed for structural effect and to frame a view. The lilac had been thinned and opened up to afford views through the plant to the water, making the water view even more dramatic.

Plants with interesting natural forms can also be used for sculptural effect — weeping plants, plants with twisted branching habits and strong fastigiate shapes. In winter when the branches are bare, the structure of these plants can be much more fully appreciated. You might want to select a few strongly sculptural plants for key locations.

Weeping beech (*Fagus sylvatica* 'Pendula') with its strongly arching branches becomes especially beautiful in winter. When branches are covered with a thin coating of ice, sun and wind make the plant seem to sparkle and dance. While such a moment can be fleeting, when it happens the plant is transformed into a gigantic crystal chandelier. Harry Lauder's walking-stick (*Corylus avellana* 'Contorta') is largely unremarkable in summer when foliage masks the twisted branches. As the autumn winds rip away the final leaves the bones of the plant become a distinctive sculptural piece. I remember an unusual hedge of this plant. Underlit with night-lighting, it became a fence of sculptural twigs casting fantastic shadows.

Plants of distinctive form are most effective when placed along a walkway, driveway or other well traveled route in wintertime or when viewed from a favorite window.

Nightlighting

Among the negative aspects of winter are the long nights with the dark pressing against the glass and the wind rattling the windowpanes. Hence, nightlighting is one of the most useful devices for the winter garden. Adding just one or two lights can extend the view outward to a tree, wall, fence or piece of sculpture. Lights can lengthen the viewing time, accent a plant or plants or silhouette plant structure.

Gardeners typically do not appreciate the possibilities of strategically placed lights. Most people rely on spotlights mounted on a wall or near the roofline to flood the lawn and garden with light. But garden lighting should be subtle and you should never be able to see the source of light. The desired effect is gentle highlighting, not blinding brightness.

It's easy to experiment with lighting yourself. Inexpensive plastic holders for spotlights intended for outdoor use are available at garden centers. Fit the holders with spotlights and spend an evening experimenting in your garden. Have a number of outdoor extension cords on hand, an adaptor plug which will enable you to plug in a number of fixtures at one source and a flashlight to assist you as you move about in the dark rearranging fixtures.

Experiment by shining the light up through shrubs, backlighting the stems or trunks of trees or casting light across a fence or wall. The light can be in front of the plant, behind it at ground level or high up in the plant itself. The light can aim upward or downward. I often use small nails to temporarily hold the light fixture in the tree. As you light a plant, look at it from many angles but especially from the point which will be the primary view. The experimenting can occur over a period of time so that you can carefully evaluate the effect.

There are many kinds of lighting fixtures and bulbs; a professional lighting consulant can advise you about the options. Once you've found a lighting effect that's to your liking, you can have an electrician wire it permanently into place.

One of the nicest things about a winter-time garden is that there are no weeds to worry about, insects are few and far between and there is little in the way of staking, deadheading and other chores. The winter garden is a relaxed and tranquil — and with a bit of imagination, visually and spatially exciting — place.   ✳

TREES AND SHRUBS FOR WINTER INTEREST

BY TIM BOLAND

CHRISTINE M. DOUGLAS

There is no thing in nature finer and
stronger than the bark of a tree;
it is a thing in place, adapted to its
ends, perfect in its conformation,
beautiful in its color and its form and
the sweep of its contour; and every
bark is peculiar to its species.

Liberty Hyde Bailey
The Holy Earth, 1915
Charles Scribners & Sons, New York

Gardeners often seek out plants that signal the beginning or the end of a season. For example, many covet the cheerfulness of ornamental cherries blooming in the wake of the first warm days of spring,

TIM BOLAND *is the Nursery Manager/Plant Propagator at Michigan State University, which includes the Beal Botanic Garden. He graduated from MSU with a B.S. in Landscape Horticulture, worked as an intern at the Scott Arboretum and was a fellow at Wisley, the garden of the Royal Horticultural Society of England.*

Woody plants with exceptional form or bark add drama to the winter landscape. Above is the native Canadian hemlock, *Tsuga canadensis.*

or a shade tree that becomes a blaze of crimson in fall, marking the end of another growing year. However, there are a number of trees and shrubs that save their best performance for winter.

Too many gardeners rely on evergreens to provide color in the winter landscape. While I don't dismiss their use, I maintain that there are also many deciduous plants that add interest to the winter garden. By selecting plants with exceptional form, structure or bark homeowners can add color and beauty to the winter landscape and increase the garden's year-round appeal. Whether a large specimen

Acer griseum, paperbark maple.

17

smaller trees and shrubs, the possi-
s are endless. I've compiled the fol-
g list of trees and shrubs with fellow
western gardeners foremost in mind,
t many are also suitable for gardens
roughout the East.

Some of the most majestic native trees
for winter drama are the North American
oaks. In general, they become large trees
with strong, stout branches. The white
oak, *Quercus alba*, the largest and longest
living species oak in North America,
develops into a magnificent tree with long,
thick, horizontal branches coming from a
sturdy trunk to form a broad rounded
crown. It strikes an imposing silhouette
against a bright winter sky. The bur oak,
Quercus macrocarpa, a heavy branched
tree with a large gray trunk and ascending
branches, assumes a rugged character in
the winter garden. The roughened twigs
have broad corky wings which add additional interest. The chestnut oak, *Quercus
muehlenbergii*, another oak with an exceptional form, develops into a medium size
tree with attractive, brownish-white, flaky
bark. Its sweet acorns are treasured by
humans and wildlife alike.

RECOMMENDED TREES AND SHRUBS

SPECIES	COMMON NAME	SIZE
Acer buergerianum	Trident Maple	M
A. capillipes		S
A. griseum	Paperbark maple	M
A. pensylvanicum	Striped bark maple	M
A. triflorum	Three flower maple	M
A. truncatum	Shantung maple	M
Aesculus octandra	Yellow buckeye	L
(syn. *A. flava*)		
Amelanchier x *grandiflora*		M
A. arborea	Downy serviceberry	M
A. canadensis	Shadblow	S
Betula alleghaniensis	Alleghany birch	L
B. lenta	Sweet birch	M
B. lutea	Yellow birch	L
B. nigra	River birch	L
B. nigra 'Heritage'	Heritage river birch	L
B. papyrifera	Paper bark birch	L
B. platyphylla var.		
japonica 'Whitespire'	Whitespire birch	M
Carpinus betulus	European hornbeam	M

A member of the oak family which is often overlooked is the American beech. Commonly found in native forests, it is less common in the cultivated landscape. Like some of the larger oaks, the American beech demands a big open space. Given ample room it will become a massive, yet graceful, tree with smooth gray bark and wide spreading branches. (Unfortunately for this native giant, the smooth gray bark provides an enticing surface for tree carvers and graffiti artists.)

While these large trees are worth seeking out and planting, they require large spaces and many years to develop. For many gardens a small or medium size tree is a more suitable choice. The river birch, *Betula nigra*, found along streams and in wet areas in the wild, has a flaky whitish-brown to cinnamon-brown exfoliating bark. At maturity it will reach 30 to 50 feet with a rounded crown. Because the degree of exfoliating bark varies from tree to tree, it is best to purchase trees that already exhibit showy bark. An exceptional cultivar, 'Heritage', has handsome peeling bark and dark green foliage. An attractive land-

SPECIES	COMMON NAME	SIZE
C. caroliniana	American hornbeam	M
C. japonica	Japanese hornbeam	M
Carya ovata	Shagbark hickory	L
Celtis occidentalis	Hackberry	L
Chionanthus retusus	Chinese fringetree	M
C. viriginicus	Fringe tree	M
Cladrastis lutea	Yellowwood	L
Cornus alba 'Sibirica'	Tatarian dogwood	S
C. alternifolia	Pagoda dogwood	S
C. controversa	Giant dogwood	L
C. kousa	Kousa dogwood	M
C. mas	Cornelian cherry	M
C. officinalis	Japanese cornel	M
C. racemosa	Gray dogwood	S
C. sanguinea 'Viridissima'	Blood twig dogwood	S
C. sericea 'Cardinal'	Red osier dogwood	S
C. sericea 'Flaviramea'		S
C. sericea 'Isanti'		S
C. sericea 'Sibirica'		S
C. sericea 'Silver and Gold'		S
Corylus colurna	Turkish filbert	L
Cotinus obovatus	American smoke tree	M
Diospyros virginiana	Persimmon	L
Evodia danielii	Korean evodia	L

(Continued on page 22)

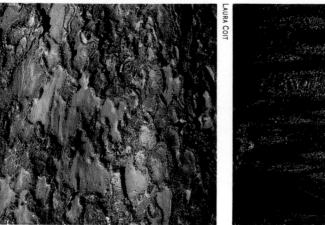

Ulmus parvifolia,
Chinese elm.

Prunus serrulata,
Japanese flowering cherry.

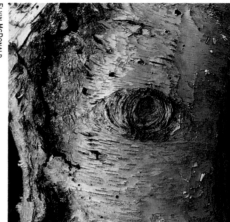

Salix x sepulcralis,
weeping willow

Betula maximowicziana,
monarch birch.

scape feature throughout the growing season, exfoliating or peeling bark is most prominent in the winter landscape. One of the most sought after trees for its bark is the paperbark maple, *Acer griseum.* A small to medium size tree, it has beautiful reddish-brown bark that begins to curl and peel at an early age. In full sun with a moist, well-drained soil, this maple develops into an unrivaled specimen tree. A Michigan garden gave me my most vivid impression of this tree: a beautiful thirty-year-old specimen accented by a soft green carpet of the allegheny spurge, *Pachysandra procumbens,* at its base. The paperbark maple is difficult to propagate and therefore usually expensive.

Another choice medium size tree, with mottled bark, is the lacebark elm, *Ulmus parvifolia.* Lacebark is a descriptive term

Betula nigra,
river birch.

Cornus alba 'Sibirica',
red-barked dogwood.

Rubus biflorus,
Himalayan bramble.

Cornus sericea 'Flaviramea',
golden-twig dogwood.

for the beautiful contrasts of orange and brown flakes that appear on its trunk and branches. This elm performs well in tough urban situations and makes an exceptional shade tree in the summer months. It is also resistant to the Dutch elm disease that devasted our most graceful native, the American elm.

Some of our beautiful native understory trees also make fine selections for the win-ter garden. The striped bark maple, *Acer pensylvanicum*, is a small tree with a jade-green trunk marked with soft white stria-tions. Plant this species in a woodland situation in filtered light; like many wood-land plants, it thrives in a spot that closely mimics its native habitat. It does not per-form well in full sun as a specimen in a lawn. A closely related species, *Acer capil-lipes*, is native to Japan and has a similarly striped bark. It too should be planted in a protected site, not in full sun.

The shadblow, *Amelanchier canadensis*, which blooms in early spring, is also a graceful addition to the winter garden. This multistemmed shrub or small tree spreads by suckering from its base, forming a mass of smooth gray branches subtly marked with dark gray and white striations. A native woodland plant, it thrives in full sun. *Amelanchier arborea*, the downy serviceberry, is similar in appearance but at maturity is more treelike and has a far greater spread.

Shrubs like yews and junipers which are planted to provide evergreen color in the winter landscape are complemented by shrubs with colorful stems that offer a striking contrast. There are several *Cornus* selections which are noteworthy for their brightly colored stems including 'Viridissima', 'Sibirica' and 'Isanti' with blood red twigs, and 'Flaviramea' with greenish-yellow stems. All of these combine well with other plants in a mixed border. Because new or one-year-old stems are the most colorful, it is important to prune out the older wood that is losing

SPECIES	COMMON NAME	SIZE
E. hupehensis	Hupeh evodia	L
Fagus grandifolia	American beech	L
F. sylvatica	European beech	L
Gymnocladus dioica	Kentucky coffee tree	L
Halesia carolina	Carolina silverbell	L
H. monticola	Mountain silverbell	L
Hovenia dulcis	Japanese raisin tree	M
Hydrangea anomala subsp. *petiolaris*	Clinging hydrangea	vine
H. quercifolia	Oakleaf hydrangea	S
Liquidambar styraciflua	Sweetgum	L
Maackia amurensis	Amur maackia	L
M. chinensis	Chinese maackia	M
Magnolia acuminata	Cucumber tree	L
Metasequoia glyptostroboides	Dawn redwood	L
Nyssa sylvatica	Tupelo tree	L
Ostrya virginiana	American hop hornbeam	M
Parrotia persica	Persian ironwood	M
Phellodendron amurense	Corktree	L
Prunus maackii	Amur chokecherry	L
P. sargentii	Sargent cherry	M
P. serrula		M
P. subhirtella 'Pendula'	Weeping higan cherry	M

color. Pruning also encourages new growth. Two recent introductions include 'Cardinal', with cherry-red stems, and 'Silver and Gold' , with yellow stems and elegant variegated foliage during the growing season.

A more subtle dogwood is *Cornus racemosa*, the gray dogwood. In the winter the bare stems, soft gray at the base and topped by the chestnut brown of the previous season's growth, make a beautiful display when the sun shines on them. Commonly found growing with deciduous hollies in wetland sites, the gray dogwood also tolerates dry or poor soils.

These are just a few of the many plants that can add depth and continuity to your year-round garden. While many of these plants are readily available, some will be difficult to locate but worth pursuing. Take time to visit local botanic gardens, arboreta or natural areas during the winter months to study these and other possibilities. To insure that trees readily adapt to your backyard environment, purchase them from nurseries that produce them from seed collected in your area.   ❄

Species	Common name	Size
Quercus bicolor	Swamp white oak	L
Q. macrocarpa	Bur oak	L
Q. muehlenbergii	Chestnut oak	L
Rubus biflorus		S
R. cockburnianus		S
Salix 'Golden Curls'		S
S. 'Scarlet Curls'		S
S. alba 'Britzensis'		S
S. alba 'Vitellina'		S
S. chaenomeloides		S
S. irrorata		S
S. melanostachys	Black pussy willow	S
Sassafras albidum	Common sassafras	M
Sorbus alnifolia	Korean mountain ash	L
Stewartia pseudocamellia	Japanese stewartia	M
Syringa pekinensis	Peking lilac	M
S. reticulata	Japanese tree lilac	M
Taxodium distichum	Bald cypress	L
Tilia petiolaris	Pendent silver linden	L
T. tomentosa	Silver linden	L
Ulmus parvifolia	Lacebark zelkova	L
Zelkova serrata	Japanese zelkova	L

DECIDUOUS HOLLIES

BY ANDREW BUNTING

Deciduous hollies are stars in the winter garden. During the winter months they provide orange and red berries.* These waxy fruits cover the naked branches and persist for weeks.

Deciduous hollies are members of the genus *Ilex*. They are related to the more common evergreen hollies, like the American holly, *Ilex opaca,* and the English holly, *Ilex aquifolium*, but their leaves are thinner, spineless and deciduous. A number of species are valued as ornamentals, including *I. verticillata, I. serrata* and *I. decidua*.

Ilex verticillata, also called winterberry, and black alder or Michigan holly and its

* The fruit of deciduous hollies is technically a berrylike rounded drupe; in this article we use the common term berry.

ANDREW BUNTING *is Curator of Plants at Chanticleer, a 32-acre private garden in Wayne, Pennsylvania which will soon open to the public. He previously worked at the Scott Arboretum and at Tintinhull House in England.*

hybrids, from crosses of *I. verticillata* with *I. serrata*, are some of the most attractive deciduous hollies. The hybrids combine the large orange to red fruits of *I. verticillata* with the smaller, darker but more abundant fruits of *I. serrata*. What results are outstanding selections that fruit heavily. These hollies adapt well to a wide range of growing conditions. In the wild, *I. verticillata* grows in low woodlands and along river bottoms from Nova Scotia to Wisconsin and south to Florida. At the Scott Arboretum in Swarthmore, Pennsylvania, they thrive and produce many fruits under hot, dry conditions. Deciduous hollies don't suffer from any serious pest or disease problems. Cold hardiness is another virtue: While most hollies are hardy only to USDA zone 5 (-10 to 20 degrees F), many of the deciduous hollies are hardy to zone 3 (-30 to -40 degrees F).

For optimal growth, plant deciduous hollies in full sun to partial shade, in acid soil that is high in organic matter. A pH of 4.5 to 6 is best as they may develop chlorotic leaves if the pH is too high.

Ilex verticillata 'Shaver'. While most hollies are hardy only to USDA zone 5, many deciduous hollies are hardy to zone 3. The waxy fruits persist for weeks.

The only maintenance these hollies require is selective thinning of branches. Deciduous hollies expand by stoloniferous underground stems and as they mature they often form thickets. Pruning to thin out the older branches will encourage young vigorous growth.

Once the proper growing environment has been established there are a number of effective ways to display deciduous hollies. A dramatic combination that may appeal to native plant enthusiasts is *Ilex verticillata* with its bright red berries and *Hamamelis virginiana* with its yellow flowers, planted against a background of dark evergreen arborvitae, *Thuja occidentalis*. Equally striking is the effect of intertwining an espalier against a stone wall, of *I.* x 'Sparkleberry', (a cross of *I. verticillata* and *I. serrata*) with its brilliant dark red berries, and *Hamamelis mollis* 'Pallida', with sulphur-yellow flowers. For beautiful combinations of color in fall, use deciduous hollies in combination with other ornamentals that exhibit showy fruits like the sapphire berry, *Symplocos paniculata*, beautyberry, *Callicarpa dichotoma, C. japonica,* or *C. bodinieri* 'Profusion' and the purple chokeberry, *Aronia prunifolia*.

Deciduous hollies planted in front of an evergreen background brighten up even the darkest corner of the winter garden. Good background plants include the dark green *Thuja, Chamaecyparis, Ilex glabra* and golden *Chamaecyparis obtusa* 'Crippsii', or for a blue-green background try an *Abies* or *Picea* sp. Using deciduous hollies for an informal hedge is an effective alternative to the ubiquitous burning bush, *Euonymus alatus*. Dwarf cultivars of these hollies such as *I. verticillata* 'Red Sprite' and *I.* x 'Hopewell Myte' make good foundation plantings. Masses of deciduous hollies in fruit become even brighter when covered with a fresh layer of snow.

My favorite deciduous hollies are the dark red, heavy fruiting selections like *I.* x 'Sparkleberry'. Its branches are covered with glossy dark red berries that contrast with its dark green foliage as the berries turn from green to red in September. Persisting longer than most deciduous hollies, their colorful fruits provide an effective display well into March. *Ilex verticillata* 'Winter Red' is another choice cultivar with dark red fruits. While many selections of *I. verticillata* and *I. serrata* x *verticillata* may reach up to 12 feet, 'Winter Red' matures at six to eight feet, making it well suited for smaller gardens. Unlike other cultivars that must reach a certain age before they produce an effective fruit display, 'Winter Red' begins fruiting as a three year old.

Another deciduous holly that is well suited to the small garden is 'Red Sprite' growing to only three feet. At the Scott Arboretum a group of 'Red Sprite' is planted near the base of a *Betula pendula*. The red fruit against the white bark makes for a colorful winter scene. Due to be released in the 1990s is the smallest holly of this type, 'Hopewell Myte', a dwarf descendant of 'Sparkleberry'. It produces an abundance of red fruit and after ten years is only two feet high.

Also worthy of consideration, with long lasting, bright red fruits, are *I.* x 'Harvest Red' and 'Autumn Glow'. 'Tiasquam' has large red fruits that are set off by its rich dark green foliage. A good upright form, 'Cacapon' arches under the weight of its fruits.

If you don't like the true red-fruited deciduous hollies there are more subtle orange-red fruited cultivars. Although production may be sparse, *I. verticillata* 'Earlibright's' fruits are large, one-half inch in diameter. 'Bright Horizon' has a bushy habit and produces an abundance of berries and dark green foliage. 'Fairfax', another heavy fruiter, has purple fall foliage. *Ilex verticillata* 'Sunset' has a spreading form and 'Afterglow' is a small holly with glossy leaves, reaching six feet in height. A cultivar with fruits that are a true orange is 'Aurantiaca', but they do not persist and as they age they fade to a yellow-orange.

Yellow-fruited cultivars are rare in the nursery trade but a few are available, including *Ilex verticillata* 'Winter Gold'. A branch sport of 'Winter Red', it, too, is a good choice for the small garden. A yellow-fruited form of the native *Ilex verticillata*, var. *chrysocarpa*, discovered in the wilds of Massachusetts, is a good yellow but does not produce the abundance of fruit that the red forms do.

A deciduous holly with a treelike habit, *Ilex decidua*, the possumhaw, exhibits a range of colorful berries that vary from yellow to red. At maturity it will reach 15 feet, with an umbrellalike habit. Like other deciduous hollies, it will grow in full sun or partial shade. Unlike *I. verticillata* which develops chlorosis if the soil pH is too high, *I. decidua* will tolerate alkaline soils. 'Warren's Red' is considered to be the best selection of the possumhaw. A large upright plant, its dark green foliage is replaced in fall by an abundance of bright red fruits. Other outstanding cultivars for red fruits include: 'Reed', 'Sentry', 'Red Escort', 'Pocahontas' and 'Red Cascade' which is a large plant with silvery, wavy branches.

Both 'Council Fire' and 'Sundance' have orange-red berries and a compact habit, growing to seven feet high by six feet wide after nine years. For showy yellow fruits try 'Byers Golden', with berries that persist until February. 'Gold Finch' is also available.

The Japanese equivalent to the native American deciduous hollies is *Ilex serrata*, also called the fine-tooth holly or Japanese winterberry. Like other deciduous hollies it too thrives in both wet and dry sites. In the wilds of Japan and China it grows in wet areas. This holly has many positive attributes. An abundant fruiter, its one-quarter-inch berries are the darkest red (blood red) of any of the deciduous hollies, making it a valued species for holly breeding programs. Under cultivation it rarely exceeds eight feet in height, providing another choice plant for the small garden. *I. decidua* 'Leucocarpa', often sold as a white fruiting form although the fruits are more of a pale yellow, is worth seeking out. A selection with tiny yellow fruits that cover its branches is 'Xanthocarpa'. An unusual dwarf selection with very small leaves and berries, a twisted, twiggy habit and new growth that is a rich purple is 'Koshobai'. The most suitable use for this holly is as a bonsai specimen.

There is also an assortment of native American hollies, not as well known, which include *I. collina*, considered by some to be a species of *Nemopanthus*. *I. collina* 'Mary Randolph' and 'Mary Staggers' are selections with red berries. Also a native, *Ilex longipes*, the Georgia longstalk holly, has red fruits borne on pendulous pedicels. 'Natchez Belle' is a select form of this species. The native *Ilex amelanchier* has small velvety red fruits.

All hollies are dioecious, which means

that plants bear either male or female flowers. Only female plants will produce fruit, but for fruiting to occur there must be a male in the vicinity to pollinate the female flowers. (One male is needed for every 10 to 20 females. A male plant can be planted in the back of a mass planting or in a separate part of the garden; within 50 feet of the females is best.) Bees are the chief pollinator for hollies. For the hybrids that are the result of crosses of *I. serrata* and *I. verticillata*, which include 'Sparkleberry', 'Autumn Glow', 'Bonfire' and 'Harvest Red', good pollinators are 'Apollo' or 'Raritan Chief'. For selections of *I. decidua* and *I. serrata*, the male species of either type can be used for a pollinator. For *I. verticillata* and its cultivars, two outstanding male cultivars are available. Both *I. verticillata* 'Quansoo'

and *I. verticillata* 'Jackson' produce large amounts of pollen. 'Jackson' has the added benefit of purple foliage in the fall, making it the more desirable choice. Males of the American holly, *Ilex opaca,*can also serve as pollinators for cultivars of *Ilex verticillata*.

The easiest method of propagation is from cuttings. Softwood cuttings, four to five inches long, taken from June to July and treated with 7,500 ppm IBA quick dip or talc (trade brands include Hormodin # 3 or Rootone), placed in a peat/perlite mix with mist will root in six to eight weeks. Starting from seed is impractical because germination takes up to a year.

The ripe and colorful berries of deciduous hollies mark the end of the growing season and enable gardeners to enjoy a winter landscape ablaze with color. ❄

Above: *Ilex* 'Harvest Red'. Plant deciduous hollies in full sun to partial shade in acid soil that is rich in organic matter.

Miscanthus 'Zebrinus' strikes a sculptural pose in the winter garden.

ORNAMENTAL GRASSES
FOR THE WINTER LANDSCAPE

BY RICK DARKE

Many ornamental grasses are at their best in winter. Intricately detailed yet surprisingly sturdy, the dramatic flower heads often become even more attractive after being dried and brightened

RICK DARKE'S *work as Longwood Gardens' curator of plants has taken him around the world in search of new plants for American gardens. His special interests include native American plants and ornamental grasses, both native and exotic. His home garden in Pennsylvania features wildflowers and grasses.*

by the autumn sun. The leaves of some are evergreen, adding welcome greens or subtle blues to the winter landscape. Others dry to winter hues of chestnut, almond, russet and fawn. These light colors can be dramatically set off by a backdrop of dark green conifers, or they can be used to provide contrast for colorful bark such as that of paperbark maple, *Acer griseum,* or *Prunus serrula,* or bright berries such as the red winterberry holly, *Ilex verticillata.* As in summer, the winter winds play with the grasses, bringing movement and sound to this potentially still, silent season. The winter beauty of the grasses is accentuated by a light coating of snow, and an ice storm can turn seedheads into glistening jewels.

Maintenance is a relatively simple matter of cutting back old growth once a year, plus occasionally lifting and dividing clumps. Most true grasses (members of the grass family, Gramineae) prefer sunny spots in the garden, although they are otherwise adapted to a wide range of soil and moisture conditions, and are relatively disease-free. The following grasses are among the best for the winter garden. Chosen for their length of interest and ease of maintenance, all are reliably cold-hardy through zone 5, unless otherwise noted.

The genus *Andropogon* includes a number of North American native species well suited to naturalistic winter gardens. All are sturdy enough to withstand repeated snows, and their colors generally last through winter into spring. Broomsedge, *Andropogon virginicus,* is perhaps best known for the rich orange color of its winter foliage. The flowers are small but numerous, occurring in clusters along the upright stems, and glow in the sun. Best used in masses or sweeps in dry sun, as it occurs naturally, broomsedge is hardy into zone 3. The winter color of bushy beardgrass, *Andropogon glomeratus,* is more salmon, and the flowers are clustered near the top of the stem, surrounded by broad leaf sheaths. Slightly shorter but more substantial than broomsedge, this species is effective in masses or as a specimen. Naturally adapted to wet sites, it is easily grown in drier garden soils, and is hardy into zone 4. Elliot's broomsedge, *Andropogon elliotii,* is similar, but the leaf sheaths surrounding the flowers are fewer, broader and deep orange in color. The foliage of *Andropogon ternarius* turns purple-red in fall, and remains colorful long into winter. The

upright flowering stems are among the showiest of the beardgrasses. Big bluestem, *Andropogon gerardii,* generally deteriorates by December and is not effective in the winter garden.

Karl Foerster's feather-reed grass, *Calamagrostis* x *acutiflora* 'Karl Foerster', grows five feet tall and is treasured for its narrow, upright flower plumes, which are effective from June through March. It performs well in full sun or light shade, and is equally effective as a single specimen or in a huge sweep. Fine textured but sturdy enough to withstand moderate snows, it is hardy through zone 4. A sterile hybrid, it is easily propagated by division in spring or fall.

Korean feather-reed grass, *Calamagrostis arundinacea* var. *brachytricha,* is quite different from the preceding. Preferring light shade, this species is more lax in habit, producing broader terminal flower clusters that remain into January.

Wild-oat, *Chasmanthium latifolium,* is one of the finest grasses for winter interest. Growing three to four feet tall, it is adapted to full sun or as much as half shade, and is cold-hardy through zone 4. The attractive oatlike flower clusters are nearly one inch long. Suspended at the ends of gracefully arching branches, they are attractive from early July until the following spring, and make excellent cut flowers. Wild-oat is effective as a specimen or in mass, and is sturdy enough to withstand heavy snows and ice. It has a tendency to self sow; however, it is easily managed.

It is easy to understand why true pampas grass *Cortaderia selloana,* has often been overused from zone 8, south, where it is reliably cold-hardy. Often exceeding ten feet in height, pampas grass produces huge feathery plumes above the basal foliage, which is evergreen in warmer zones. The plumes last through the winter and are superb in dried arrangements. Variegated cultivars such as 'Goldband', which has yellow-striped leaves, are effective year-round in southernmost zones. Smaller in stature and less a Victorian icon, the cultivar 'Pumila' is more suited to smaller, modern gardens and is often hardy into zone 7.

No other grass can rival the lofty winter display of ravenna grass, *Erianthus ravennae,* a native of southern Europe. Giant reed, *Arundo donax,* is equal in height but generally deteriorates by November, offering little winter interest. Ravenna grass is often used in place of pampas grass in cold climates, since it is reliably hardy through zone 6 and into zone 5. In late summer, the large flower plumes open on straight stems, towering nearly 15 feet above the basal foliage. Ravenna grass always remains attractive through January, and in mild winters it is still effective into March. The genus *Erianthus* also includes a number of little-known North American natives that hold great promise for the winter garden. They are generally much smaller than ravenna grass, ranging from six to nine feet in height, and are more in scale with modest residential gardens. Bent-awn plume grass, *Erianthus contortus,* is bolt-upright, to six feet tall. Its rich orange-red fall foliage color persists through most of winter, and the sturdy flower stems will still be standing in late March. It prefers full sun. Silver plume grass, *Erianthus alopecuroides,* is similar but lacks the reddish winter color. It is adapted to shady sites.

Most ornamental fescues, *Festuca* spp., are evergreen or semievergreen even in colder climates, and can add significant interest to the winter garden. Most commonly available are various blue or blue-green leaved cultivars of *Festuca ovina* and *Festuca cinerea,* which are usually no more than eight inches tall. They are hardy in zone 4, and will remain attractive nearly year-round if provided excellent drainage. Growing one foot in height but similar in blue-foliage effect is *Festuca amethystina* 'Superba'. Atlas fescue, *Festuca mairei,* makes an elegant two-foot-tall mound of gray-green foliage. For milder climates there are excellent blue-leaved forms of California fescue, *Festuca californica.*

Blue oat grass, *Helictotrichon sempervirens,* is among the best of the blue-leaved grasses for winter. Cold hardy to zone 5 and fully evergreen in zones 8 south, it produces a 16-inch tuft of fine-textured foliage. Good drainage is a must.

As a group, the various cultivars of *Miscanthus sinensis,* are hard to beat for winter interest. Most prefer full sun; however, they tolerate a wide range of soil and moisture conditions. Although most of these large grasses go fully dormant, their bold foliage and flower heads are sturdy and persistent, having more presence in the winter garden than any deciduous shrub. The flower heads may be cut through the winter for use in dried arrangements. Winter foliage color is usually a pleasing light beige. If left standing, miscanthus will begin to shed leaves by early winter, necessitating a certain amount of clean-up if the desire is to keep the garden "litter-free." The winter beauty of these plants more than justifies this minimal amount of care. After all, is it reasonable to expect the winter garden to be a "no-maintenance" garden?

Not surprisingly, miscanthus cultivars that flower later in the season remain attractive longer into winter. Many are still in good shape in late March, when they should be cut back before new growth begins. 'Gracillimus' and 'Sarabande' both have fine-textured green summer foliage, and stand up well through winter storms. 'Morning Light' is similarly fine-textured and durable, with white-striped summer

The bold foliage and flower heads of the various *Miscanthus* cultivars have more presence in the winter garden than deciduous shrubs.
Above: *Miscanthus sinensis* 'Gracillimus'.

foliage. Of all the broad-leaved white-variegated types, the recent introduction 'Cosmopolitan' is sturdiest and longest-lasting in the winter garden, far surpassing the old-fashioned 'Variegatus'. As for the gold-banded cultivars, 'Strictus' is sturdier in winter than 'Zebrinus'. The more diminutive cultivars 'Yaku Jima' and 'Adagio' hold up well. 'Purpurascens' is best known for its orange-red fall color, and the dormant foliage retains an attractive reddish cast into late winter.

Growing four to five feet tall, our North American native switch grass, *Panicum virgatum,* remains attractive and upright throughout winter, even when there is considerable snowfall. Of the available cultivars, 'Heavy Metal', which is blue-leaved in summer, is the most strictly upright.

The flowers of hardy fountain grass, *Pennisetum alopecuroides,* are generally past peak by November, however the foliage, especially that of the low-growing cultivar 'Hameln', can make an effective groundcover through February.

Little bluestem, *Schizachyrium scoparium,* is finer textured but similar in most aspects to *Andropogon,* in which it was once included. Although best for naturalized groups or masses, its orange-red winter color can be very satisfying against a winter snow.

The genus *Sesleria* includes a number of evergreen or semievergreen species of

Miscanthus sinensis 'Gracillimus' holds up well through winter storms. In late March, it should be cut back before new growth begins.

merit in the winter garden. *Sesleria autumnalis* produces a tufted mound of light green foliage 16 inches tall, which retains its color through most of winter. It prefers light shade, and is suited to groundcover massing. The leaves of *Sesleria heufleriana* are blue-green, also to 16 inches tall. The curious dark brown to black flowers rise out of the foliage in early March, providing late winter interest.

Indian grass, *Sorghastrum nutans, is* another North American native with considerable winter interest. Upright in habit and five to seven feet tall, its foliage and flowerheads remain attractive into February. Of the blue-leaved prairie types, the cultivar 'Sioux Blue' is the sturdiest and most upright though winter. Indian grass is hardy through zone 4.

Little known but readily available, Japanese themeda, *Themeda japonica*, offers unique sculptural interest in the winter garden. The stems radiate in a dramatic arc five feet tall, and although delicate in appearance, they usually stand up through January, sometimes into March.

Purple-top, *Tridens flavus,* is best known for the "purple top" it puts on local old-fields and meadows in late summer. This native clump former is spare and open, but its delicate flower panicles can be exquisite when covered by a winter frost or a thin mantle of ice. They remain standing through winter and into the following spring. ❄

HERBACEOUS PLANTS

FOR THE WINTER GARDEN

BY JOANNA REED

Here in Pennsylvania, winter is a season to enjoy gazing through frosted windows from the warmth of a cozy room, or walking on crunchy leaves dusted with snow.

During my childhood winter was exciting only when white with snow, enough to cloak the gloomy barrenness, enough for sledding and snowballs. Snow always brings smiles to winter sports enthusiasts. But gardeners also smile as deep snow provides cover from drying winds and scorching sun.

With or without snow, winter took on new dimensions as I attended classes at the Arboretum of the Barnes Foundation in Merion, Pennsylvania. As I toured the Arboretum weekly, I became aware of patterns ranging from the light filigree of

JOANNA REED *has been growing plants at her garden, Longview Farm in Malvern, Pennsylvania for more than 50 years. A past president of the Herb Society of America, her garden features a large variety of herbaceous plants and was featured in* The American Woman's Garden.

deciduous branches to stark verticals of tree trunks and colors ranging from the ghostly grays to browns that are almost black. Bark was splotched, striped and exfoliating, diverse and interesting and there were greens of all conceivable shades. Shape, texture, sun and air movement, as well as size, determined how these greens appeared. Evergreens — trees and shrubs, needled and broadleaved, solid green or variegated — contrasted with and enhanced one another.

Deciduous plants added lightness. Fruits in clusters or single provided dashes of color. On the ground a tapestry of foliage, green, bronze, gray and mauve intermingled with dried furled leaves and stones, some bare, others covered with soft green mosses.

Those shivery winter walks at the Barnes Arboretum engendered great enthusiasm and made me more aware of the local vegetation. The farm fields and dividing hedgerows provided a pleasant rhythm. An occasional lone cedar, *Juniperus virginiana*, or black alder, *Ilex verticillata*, provided contrast and sparkle. The wooded acres were also influential in the planning and planting of my own garden, a process that has been going on for close to 50 years.

The trees that were under two feet tall when I planted them now provide vertical interest, serve as focal points and shelter spaces and buildings: *Cercidiphyllum japonicum*, magnolias, *Paulownia tomentosa, Styrax japonicus, Cornus florida, Cornus kousa, Cornus mas, Ilex opaca* and *Cryptomeria*. A mass planting of swamp maples, ash, *Amelanchier canadensis, Liquidambar styraciflua* and *Nyssa sylvatica* screens from view a highway, and merges into a softened right angle with the existing woods.

These trees, underplanted with shrubs, serve as backgrounds for herbaceous borders, and as dividers to create rooms. Trees and shrubs were selected to provide winter interest and color, as well as blooms and shade. Herbaceous plants unite them into distinct landscape masses and tie them to the earth.

First I planted the area between shrubs and under trees with bulbs. For groundcovers I planted vinca, pachysandra and ivy. The ivy proved too willing to climb all and everything, making it too vigorous and labor intensive for all but a few situations. To gain texture and height, over time I have added or replaced plants throughout the garden. Many of them are winter stars I use as edging or other features, as well as carpets.

Arum italicum appears in October. Tightly furled leaves poke through the shiny bronze mats of *Ajuga reptans* and whorls of sweet woodruff. It is odd to see a plant commence growth at such a late date. Its rich green arrow-shaped leaves overlaid with creamy white patterns are eight to12 inches long and are fresh and sprightly until late spring. The blossoms, pale yellow spathes which appear in spring, are the plain Jane cousins of better known tropical calla lily, *Zantedeschia*. The fruit (which my patch has yet to produce) is similar to jack-in-the-pulpit, spikes of orange-red berries in summer rather than fall. Fortunately, the tubers multiply and increase, as this arum is not a reliable fruit producer.

Another October lovely is *Cyclamen hederifolium*. Slender stemmed, fragile pink and white flowers appear suddenly before the foliage, which soon follows. Handsome variegated ivy-shaped leaves clothe the ground until late May when the plant goes dormant again until October. *C. hederifolium* is the hardiest cyclamen species and the easiest to grow. The stem carrying the seed capsule winds itself into a tight spring, hugs the ground until ripe, then releases and scatters the seeds some distance from the mother plant. Eventually a tuber forms that grows in size rather than dividing and multiplying like a bulb. This plant is happy among tree roots in dry shade. In my garden it has colonized under large old yews.

Helleborus foetidus, the stinking hellebore, has evergreen, narrowly lanceolate lustrous dark green foliage winter through summer. Large enough to be a featured specimen, vigorous enough to sheathe an area with interesting foliage and compliant enough to share its space with a floriferous perennial like *Begonia grandis*, it is a plant everyone should have. The flower buds form in late November, and in December open into clusters of bell-shaped chartreuse flowers. On the coldest single-digit days of winter they collapse to the ground but let the sun coax the temperature into the 20 to 30 degree F range and the hellebores are again fresh and crisp. Try a few under a February-bloom-

Cyclamen hederifolium, the hardiest
and easiest cyclamen to grow, with a
winter frosting.

Ajuga 'Burgundy Glow' forms a
handsome year-round carpet.

ing *Hamamelis mollis* or plant them
among early-blooming pale yellow primu-
las and *Viola labradorica*.

Helleborus niger, the Christmas rose, is
the next species to bloom. The foliage is
attractive all year. Large deep green,
sparsely toothed, palmate leaves enhance
the blooms. Borne singly on sturdy stems,
they are usually white, at times suffused
with pale pink. Bloom time varies with
individual plants.

Next in the sequence is *Helleborus orientalis*, the lenten rose, as lush and dark a
green most of the year as *H. niger*,
although by February and bloom time, apt
to be brown and burned. This burned

Santolina virens, gray-leaved *Artemisia ludoviciana*
and the bronze seed heads of *Sedum* 'Autumn Joy'
in the author's garden.

foliage can be clipped away. Buds emerge from the ground in great thick clusters. The flowers, two or three to a stem, reliably give a good show, ranging in color from creamy white to deep purple, including a spectrum of pinks, roses and mauves, mottled or freckled. I have seen them used stunningly to edge woodland and garden paths, enticing one to wander further into the woods. At Winterthur Garden in Delaware great drifts bloom with *Rhododendron mucronulatum, Corylopsis spicata* and an early rosy primula, a combination not soon forgotten. As the flowers of both of these species fade, all parts turn pale green and remain attractive until early summer when the ripened seeds finally scatter.

Pansies, violas and johnny-jump-ups are always ready to seize a good day by blooming. *Viola hederacea* from Australia, however, must be keeping to its "down under" schedule. The white flowers appear in November and again in March. This stoloniferous plant makes a good ground cover over small bulbs. As a hanging basket indoors, it will bloom most of the winter.

Viola labradorica, from the frozen North, also spreads into glorious mats. The undersides of the small dark green heart-shaped leaves are a lovely rich purple. The early spring flowers are small but showy. *Bergenia cordifolia* and related species, with bold leaves that lend substance to shrub and perennial borders, welcome one to a path or provide contrast in an area covered with smaller leaved plants like vinca or pachysandra. Just as welcoming is the fine foliage of *Iberis sempervirens*, or candytuft. The cultivar 'Snowflake' gives a good show of winter bloom.

Most thymes are evergreen. Ground-hugging mats or ten-inch sub-shrubs, they hold their tiny leaves until the March winds blow. Colors range from pale blue-gray to almost black-green. They are good in paving cracks, edging paths or in the front of a perennial border for winter definition.

Gray-blue dianthus with its many varieties; santolinas, both gray and green; hardy lavenders; rue and sages, especially *Salvia officinalis* 'Nana' can be used in the same fashion as thyme except in paving cracks. I have seen rue clipped into an interesting low hedge. No plant looks so dead as rue when it finally sheds its foliage. When these unlikely looking stems finally start budding out in late spring, cutting them back to the new growth will result in a stunning plant.

Another good gray, *Stachys byzantina*, surprisingly tolerant of shade as well as hot sun, moist or dry soil, retains its landscape value through the winter.

I am surprised that more people don't use *Polygonum affine* as an edging plant. Low four- to six-inch lanceolate leaves turn a rosy russet and persist all winter with seed heads poking upright like a regiment of tiny soldiers. Assuredly we are all cautious with polygonums, but this one is not as much a thug as some of its relatives, or as *Lamiastrum galeobdolon* 'Variegatum' an unexpectedly evergreen plant with attractive silver markings. *Low and creeping* the books and catalogs say; I'd say *galloping*.

Ajuga could also be called a thug but I would not be without it. Its foliage varies from a rich green with white, green with pink, green with purple and purple, pink and white. Although *Ajuga* is a spring bloomer, its foliage is handsome year-round.

The great rosettes of bright green, rough textured leaves of *Digitalis purpurea*, foxglove, lend stability as well as color. Like the hellebores, they resent it when the temperature drops to single digits but spring back dependably and continue giving pleasure. *Digitalis lutea,* with its smaller strap-like leaves and different general shape, is also a good plant for winter.

Throughout my garden are patches of young seedlings of *Silene armeria, Nigella damascena, Chrysanthemum parthenium* and *Digitalis purpurea,* which will be thinned and transplanted in spring. But for the winter they give flat washes of color on the ground.

Some seed pods I deliberately let stand until early spring. They add color and form, and bring birds to the garden — showiest is *Sedum* 'Autumn Joy', but *Baptisia australis, Physostegia, Rudbeckia, Perilla, Stachys officinalis, Iris sibirica* and some thymes all add interest through the winter months.

Working in the woods, pruning and picking up windfalls, brings me outdoors to enjoy the constant surprises and discoveries the garden offers. When the upright fronds of the Christmas fern lie close to the ground, making way for the new fiddleheads soon to come, and winter aconite and snowdrops pop out, I know spring is at hand, and December, January and February were not overly long after all.

HELLEBORES:

THE ARISTOCRATS OF WINTER-FLOWERING PLANTS

BY CHRISTOPHER WOODS

The winter garden is a showcase for texture and architecture in the landscape. The bare bones of shrubs and trees become bold and bright in the wintery sun. Flowers are rare, although precocious spring bulbs often force their way out of the cold earth to surprise us with their grace and delicacy.

We do not often think of herbaceous plants for winter — it is a time of quiescence; herbs will have their show when the world wakes. However, there are herbaceous perennials that are essential for the winter garden. Perhaps the finest are the hellebores, the Christmas rose, the Lenten rose and others.

CHRISTOPHER WOODS *is Executive Director of Chanticleer, a 32-acre private garden in Wayne, Pennsylvania, being developed as a public garden. It will open soon.*

The genus *Helleborus* includes about 20 species native to western and southern Europe, including Corsica and the Balearic Islands, and Western Asia. They belong to the buttercup family (Ranunculaceae) and have saucer-shaped, nodding flowers in subtle hues of green, white, red, pink, or purple. It is the sepals that are the most prominent part of the flower; the petals are inconspicuous.

Hellebores can be divided into two groups, those with leafy stems with flowers carried at the tip of the stems and those without stems with both leaves and flowers produced from the base of the plant.

The leaves are leathery, pale to dark green, hand-shaped and deeply divided. Used in ancient times as a purgative, hellebores contain powerful poisons. The botanical name comes from the Greek, *elein,* to injure, and *bora*, food, referring

to the posionous leaves and roots.

Hellebores require fertile and moist but reasonably well drained soil in a partly shaded site, although they are tolerant of a considerable amount of sun. They are at their best in climates with mild winters where their evergreen leaves can be seen at their finest. In areas with cold winters, the leaves often become ragged and unattractive by spring. The damaged leaves can be removed when fresh new growth appears. Most species are tolerant of cold temperatures but they benefit from snow cover or a light mulch in cold climates.

Although they should be planted in a sheltered site and left undisturbed, propagation is not impossible. Carefully divide the fleshy roots in late spring immediately after the plants have flowered. It may take up to two to three years

ABOVE: *Helleborus argutifolius*, with elegant foliage and early-spring flowers, is a comely companion to snowdrops, crocuses and the Labrador violet.

OPPOSITE, TOP: *Helleborus orientalis*, called Lenten rose because it flowers in the 40-day period before Easter, tolerates dry soil and shade.

LOWER RIGHT: *Helleborous foetidus* bears unpleasant smelling but handsome pale green, maroon-edged, bell-shaped flowers in late winter.

for the newly divided plants to establish themselves.

Like many other members of the buttercup family, hellebores are difficult to grow from seed. The seeds require up to eight weeks of high temperatures (80 degrees F) and another eight weeks of low temperatures (32 degrees F) before the temperature is raised to 40 degrees F, when the seedlings should begin to germinate. After germination, raise the temperature to about 55 degrees F. Grow plants for two years before planting in the garden.

Fortunately, many species self-sow prolifically, and thus enable gardeners to increase their supply. Seedlings often appear around the base of mature plants. Remove carefully and transplant.

Often associated with other shade plants such as ferns and hostas, hellebores are also valuable low-growing plants under deciduous trees and shrubs, particularly when grown with spring-flowering bulbs or other early flowering perennials.

Despite the number of species and hybrids, few are commonly cultivated in North America. As awareness of the enormous variety and diversity of herbaceous perennials grows, the palette of hellebores should increase.

The following is a brief description of hellebores commonly available, along with a few that deserve to be grown more widely.

The two species most commonly cultivated are the Christmas rose, *Helleborus niger*, and the Lenten rose, *Helleborus orientalis*.

Helleborus niger is native to the mountainous regions of Europe and Asia minor. It is named the Christmas rose because it often flowers around Christmas. In much of North America, however, it blooms in late winter and early spring. It is a low-growing plant, reaching about one foot in height, with a spread of 18 inches. The leaves and flowers are produced from the base of the plant. The sometimes spiny, dark green and leathery leaves are divided into seven to nine egg-shaped leaflets.

The saucer-shaped flowers, borne either singly or in pairs, are two to four inches wide and waxy white, with a central boss of yellow stamens. The flower stalk is often spotted red.

The Christmas rose is harder to grow than the Lenten rose. It needs moist but well drained neutral to alkaline soil in a partly shady site. It is sometimes susceptible to fungus diseases, particularly leafspot. The affected leaves should be removed and burned. Use fungicides only when damage to the plant is substantial. Hardy to -20 degrees F this hellebore is also tolerant of the hot and humid summers prevalent in much of North America.

A variable species, it produces forms with a variety of flower colors, sizes and bloom times. A few variants recognized by taxonomists are 'Grandiflorus', a strain with large flowers appearing in late winter and 'Praecox', with white, pink-flushed flowers blooming in early winter in mild climates. Subspecies *macranthus*, has spiny-toothed leaves and white, pink-tinged flowers borne well above the foliage. 'Allerseelen' and 'Mme Fourcade' have large pink-flushed flowers that are produced around Christmas time. 'St. Brigid' has blue-green leaves and pink-tinged flowers. 'Potter's Wheel' has large, rounded flowers with a green center.

Helleborus orientalis, the Lenten rose, so called because of its habit of flowering in the 40-day period before Easter, is a highly variable species native to Turkey and Bulgaria, growing to a height of about 18 inches and a spread of about 24 inches. The leaves, produced from the base of the plant, are coarsely serrated, glossy, long-stalked, hand-shaped and divided into 5 to 11 lobed leaflets. Two to four inches wide, the flowers are produced from winter to spring. They range in color from pure white to deep purple, often flushed pale green, blotched or speckled with dark plum-purple spots. This species is hardy to -20 degrees F and tolerant of heat although different forms may be less winter hardy and less vigorous in hot weather.

The Lenten rose is easy to cultivate in ordinary fertile soil in part to full shade. It also tolerates dry soil, making it especially useful as an herbaceous plant under trees and shrubs. There are almost 60 named forms sometimes listed as separate species, cultivars or both. Subspecies *abchasicus* has maroon spotted purple-red flowers. Subspecies *guttatus* has greenish-pink flowers spotted purple.

Variety *atrorubens* has deciduous leaves and plum-purple flowers and is one of the earliest forms to bloom. Variety *olympicus* has green flushed white flowers. There are many cultivars, most of which are currently unavailable in North America. 'Heartsease' has maroon flowers, 'Winter Cheer' has white flowers flushed pink.

Two other species are worthy of mention. *H. argutifolius*, formerly named *H. corsicus* or *H. lividus* subsp. *corsicus*, is a native of Corsica, growing to a height of two feet and a spread of two to three feet, with leaves and flowers produced on thick stems. The leaves are gray-green, conspicuously veined and divided into spiny-toothed leaflets. Fifteen to 30 pale green, cupped flowers about one inch wide are borne in clusters at the end of the flower stem in early spring. In good conditions in a mild climate this is an extraordinarily handsome plant, appealing not so much for its flowers as for its elegant foliage. It is a comely companion to snowdrops and crocuses and looks uncommonly pleasing in contrast with the dark purple leaves of the Labrador violet (*Viola labradorica*). This species has been hybridized with the Christmas rose to produce a hybrid group named *H.* x *nigericors*. One of the few commercially available cultivars, 'Alabaster', is a vigorous yet compact plant with white flowers. Not as hardy as the species already mentioned, the Corsican hellebore can sustain winter temperatures of about 0 degrees F. It is certainly not tolerant of hot weather and does not perform well in the sultry summers of the southeastern United States. It is best grown in light shade, protected from the midday sun.

H. foetidus, the stinking hellebore, is native to Western Europe, forming vigorous clumps up to 18 inches in height and spread. The leafy stems bear dark green leaves deeply divided into four to 11 narrow leaflets. The unpleasant smelling, bell-shaped flowers, one inch wide, pale green with maroon stained edges, appear in late winter and early spring in loose clusters at the end of the flower stem. This hellebore requires a neutral to alkaline, moist but well drained soil, in semishade or in sun. The pale green bells and the dark leaves make this a highly desirable plant for winter and spring display. It is slow to establish after division but self-sown seedlings are common. Hardy to about -10 degree F it also tolerates summer heat.

Flowering in the depths of winter and into spring, hellebores are a sign that winter bears life and that spring will once again arrive to restore us.   ✳

BULBS FOR
WINTER GARDENS

BY CHARLES CRESSON

The earliest spring crocus, often called snow crocus, bloom January through March, depending on climate and location. Above: *Crocus tomasinianus.*

Winter-blooming *Galanthus nivalis*, the common snowdrop,
shows unfaltering tolerance to severe frost.

Never mind the December and March solstices — gardeners define winter by temperature. Winters are longer in the north, shorter in the south. There is another difference too. The low temperatures of a northern midwinter suppress all growth, while in the South moderate temperatures allow autumn bloom to overlap with that of winter, which in turn leads into spring without interruption. Many of these same winter flowers take an enforced rest in colder climates, and bloom a month or two later. Whenever they appear, flowers braving brutal cold are an undisputed delight.

Bulbs are an essential component of winter gardens. They possess an unequaled ability to withstand hard frosts and exposure while in growth. In the South they are joined by a variety of shrubs, perennials and annuals which revel in the cool weather. Farther north, the bravest bulbs bloom alone, contributing animation to an otherwise stoic landscape of colored stems, evergreens and berries. Even as far north as zone 6 it is possible to achieve a continuous succession of bloom from fall through spring with the hardiest bulbs.

CHARLES O. CRESSON *is a professional horticulturist and writer who lives near Philadelphia. His garden is featured in* The American Man's Garden *published in 1990.*

Such hardy bulbs are snowdrops, *Galanthus*. spp. Even in the coldest spells their flowers show unfaltering tolerance to severe frost, bending to the ground, as if wilted, and recovering on the next warm day. The common snowdrop, *G. nivalis* (zone 3), blooms in February and March in my garden (zone 6) near Philadelphia, Pennsylvania, but the rarer subspecies *cilicicus* blooms as early as late December or January. Another species, *G. elwesii* (zone 4), is larger and normally seen a couple of weeks before the common snowdrop, but it is variable, and some forms are also regularly seen as early as the beginning of January. Afficionados have noticed that within the same species, different stocks may have different bloom seasons, so it pays to obtain them from several sources.

Another variable species is *Galanthus caucasicus* (zone 6). In my garden, the earliest form flowers in December, others follow in midwinter, and the latest end the season in March.

Not only do snowdrops bridge the winter season, but they also begin it. The earliest to appear is *G. nivalis* subsp. *reginae-olgae* (zones 6 or 7), sending forth their blooms and foliage as early as late October. For hardiness and bloom season, snowdrops, in all their variety, are the quintessential winter bulbs.

Though less hardy in northern climates, cyclamen surpass even snowdrops for breadth of bloom season. They are a more Southern genus and only a few are marginally hardy in my garden. (Though some do survive in protected gardens farther north.) South of Philadelphia and on the West Coast, many species of cyclamen thrive, producing a succession of pink, rose or white blooms among their winter green foliage.

Cyclamen hederifolium (zone 6) is the hardiest and easiest to grow of the species. With flowers from August to October, it hardly fits my definition of a winter-blooming species, but its ivylike foliage is attractive from September through late spring. *C. cilicium* (zone 6) seems to be as hardy and picks up the season with late fall bloom beginning in October. *C. coum* (zone 7) and its many varieties produce their first flowers around January 1st, weather permitting, and continues well into spring. It is, in my experience, the most tender of the species mentioned here and requires a very protected location. I suspect a cloche placed over it during January and February would improve its performance.

Cyclamen prefer a woodland situation. In the north, grow them under evergreen trees for protection from winter sun to help preserve the foliage. In moderate southern climates, deciduous trees serve just as well. Plant them shallowly with a light mulch.

No winter garden would be complete without crocus. They too have a wide range of bloom seasons, but since their flowers are generally more fragile than snowdrop blooms, their flowering season is confined to the autumn and spring, except in the mild winters of the South. Among the more reliable species is the October-blooming *Crocus speciosus* (zone 5) in lavender blue or white with showy orange stigmas. In mild falls, flowers continue to appear sporadically into December. A later species which clearly struggles in my garden is *C. ochroleucus* (zone 7). Its foliage gallantly appears with small white flowers in November and December, hence the leaves have a better chance of surviving the winter in warmer climates.

The earliest spring crocus appear January through March depending on the climate and location. On a southern slope here they may appear in late January, but the flowers are more successful a couple of weeks later. These are often called snow crocus and include such species as *C. tomasinianus* (zone 5), *C. chrysanthus* (zone 4), *C. sieberi* (zone 6) and *C. susianus (angustifolius)* (zone 4) in the colors of the rainbow.

Even before the earliest crocus, winter aconite, *Eranthis hyemalis* (zone 4) springs forth with bright yellow buttercup flowers held four to six inches high. When content, in rich deciduous woods, they self sow with abandon to form a sea of gold.

Late winter brings a multitude of small bulbs capable of providing masses of color. The earliest daffodil, *Narcissus asturiensis* (zone 4), often shows its golden yellow trumpets in February. It is a perfectly hardy miniature trumpet only four inches tall. A welcome companion is the pale blue *Scilla tubergeniana* (zone 5).

Next are the jewellike dwarf irises with a fragrance of violets, for those who care to kneel on a warm day. They, too, are only 4 to 6 inches tall. *Iris reticulata* and the related species *I. danfordiae* and *I. histrioides* (all zone 5) range in color from blue to purple, reddish purple, yellow and even near-white.

Carrying the display into spring are the light lavender-blue glory-of-the-snow, *Chionodoxa luciliae* (zone 3), and deep blue Siberian squill, *Scilla sibirica* (zone 2). These two grow virtually anywhere, seeding themselves without much encouragement.

Crocus tulips are so called for their short four- to six-inch stature, wide flowers and early bloom. Such similar species as *Tulipa humilis* and *T. pulchella* (both zone 4) are the first of the tulip clan to bloom

with pink or reddish flowers and yellow or black centers. They prefer full sun to do their best.

It is perfectly understandable that bulbs bloom in winter or even fall. Many bulbs originate in Mediterranean climates where inhospitable, hot, dry summers force dormancy. The cooler seasons are both moist and mild. Growth cycles begin in autumn, continue through winter and end in spring.

Many plants prefer to bloom at the beginning of the growth cycle. Competition is also reduced at this season, since larger plants have lost their leaves and winter sun comes streaming to the ground. Summer dormancy also adapts many of these bulbs to dry shade, even among tree roots where other plants struggle. Most bulbs require good drainage.

Winter bulbs are small, compared to their later-flowering counterparts, as dictated by the necessities of the season. But they are strong and vigorous, often tolerating shocking degrees of frost without permanent damage. Near the northern limit of their hardiness, those with wintergreen foliage benefit from a light covering of evergreen boughs during the coldest months.

For the best effect use these diminutive early bulbs in mass plantings. Weave them in between and among winter-blooming shrubs, hellebores and annuals such as pansies to create complete garden compositions. Low groundcovers, such as sedums and ajugas provide a green background. Winter bulbs coexist well among the roots of deciduous epimediums and hostas, filling spaces that would otherwise be bare at that season.

Used abundantly, these small bulbs bring masses of life and color to the winter landscape.   ✳

WINTER-FLOWERING TREES AND SHRUBS

BY J.C. RAULSTON

The most noted of winter-flowering woody plants are the witch-hazels, which
bloom in the dead of winter, notwithstanding severe cold and snow.
Above: *Hamamelis mollis*, Chinese witch-hazel.

JOANNE PAVIA

Hamamelis x *intermedia* 'Ruby Glow'.

JOANNE PAVIA

Hamamelis x *intermedia* 'Jelena'.

JERRY PAVIA

W hat is winter? In Minnesota and Florida, winter is vastly different, especially in terms of the plants that gardeners can grow. I will concentrate on the woody plants which perform well and flower in the mid-South Piedmont area, USDA zones 7-8, during the solar winter — December 22 to March 21 (winter solstice to spring equinox). However, many of these plants will grow in colder climates as well; check with your local nursery and Cooperative Extension office.

Why would a shrub or tree flower during this unfavorable season? Some late-fall-flowering plants continue to bloom sporadically during mild winters. Winter-flowering cherry, *Prunus subhirtella* 'Autumnalis', for example, may bloom anytime from October through March.

J.C. RAULSTON *is a Professor of Horticulture at North Carolina State University in Raleigh, North Carolina. He is also the founder of the NCSU Arboretum. His articles about plants have appeared in numerous publications, including* Horticulture.

A few other plants bloom at this same time regardless of temperature. The many witch-hazels, *Hamamelis* x *intermedia* cultivars, will bloom here and farther north even while snow is deep on the ground. Many of these true winter-flowering plants have evolved for the pollinators which are present at this time of year to ensure fertilization and seed production and therefore survival of the species. The often intense fragrance of these plants lures the pollinators. Gardeners reap the benefit.

There are also plants that will bloom when the flower buds' dormancy requirement is satisfied and the weather is warm enough for growth. Winter honeysuckle, *Lonicera fragrantissima*, is one such plant. Since this area of the South often enjoys early warm spells, this category of plants is quite important. Early flowering can also suffer from freezes that often follow, however. A classic plant in this category is the Yulan magnolia, *Magnolia denudata*. Several years ago, it was in peak bloom in mid-January — until a 15 degree freeze radically changed the scene. In my opinion, the glory of the good times is worth the agony of the occasional losses.

Many plants that bloom during brief warm spells have preformed flower buds from the previous growing season that require different degrees of chilling to break dormancy. A certain percentage of the buds open early, then another set for an entire bloom cycle. The Japanese flowering apricot, *Prunus mume,* is one example. It has bloomed as early as mid-December and it is a rare winter when the three to four weeks of blooming is not interrupted by a freeze or two. There always seems to be another set of buds for another blooming once the weather warms again.

It's ironic that a warmer than normal winter may result in less showy flower displays. With more warmth there will be fewer days of the required chilling cold that is needed to break flower bud dormancy. Warm winters may actually mean later blooming than usual.

Many experts recommended planting trees and shrubs on south-facing walls or in sunny, protected locations for winter bloom. These warmer microclimates will encourage earlier blooming, but the blossoms will also be vulnerable to frost. In their native habitat in Asia the early deciduous magnolias usually grow as understory plants in forests on north-facing slopes where cool temperatures delay flowering until frost is less likely. Gardeners must balance the benefits of the precious out-of-season bloom with the potential damage from frost. An alternative is to plant one plant in the warmest, most protected site on a property and a second in the coldest portion of the garden. This will provide insurance against damage and also lengthen the season of bloom.

Flowers are not always necessary for a beautiful and interesting display. Many species have showy winter buds which may look like flowers or can be just as striking. An example is *Skimmia japonica* 'Rubella', a two- to three-foot broad-leaved evergreen shrub which has three-inch clusters of bright red flower buds that are extremely attractive through the winter.

Two other, more commonly grown broad-leaved evergreen shrubs, *Viburnum tinus*, laurustinus, and *Pieris japonica*, Japanese pieris, also have attractive winter flower clusters — in addition to being early-blooming species. Laurustinus grows six to 12 feet high; cultivars with red buds are more showy through the winter. The flowers open white in March. Pieris, a white-flowered, three to six foot shrub, is widely grown. Among the many new cultivars are ones with red or pink winter flower buds.

The flower buds which attract the greatest attention in our garden in winter are those of *Edgeworthia papyrifera*, paper bush, a rare deciduous four- to seven-foot shrub native to Japan. The rounded heads of 30 to 40 whitish, tubelike flower buds nod from the tips of branches like small tassles in winter. They eventually open in mid-spring to two- to three-inch balls of white to yellow, slightly fragrant flowers.

The most noted of winter-flowering woody plants are the witch-hazels — six species and many hybrids of *Hamamelis*. *H.* x *intermedia* hybrids (*H. japonica* x *H. mollis*) are the showiest and most available. They are multistemmed deciduous shrubs six to 15 feet high. Over 25 cultivars with flower colors ranging from pale yellow through oranges to red are available from specialist nurseries. They always bloom in mid-winter, even in severe cold with snow.

The bright yellow flowered *H.* x *intermedia* 'Arnold Promise' is the most common cultivar, but it is among the latest of all the cultivars to bloom. For better true mid-winter flowering choose 'Primavera' (pale yellow), 'Sunburst' (bright yellow) or 'Ruby Glow' (coppery red).

The unsung hero and greatest glory of the winter-flowering woody plants is the magnificent Japanese flowering apricot, *Prunus mume*. This plant is highly revered by the Japanese who have created over 400 cultivars for their gardens, but we have yet to see them in the United States. It is a small deciduous 20-foot tree. The cultivars include a variety of plant forms — weeping, contorted and fastigiate, with single or double flowers in white through pink to red. They bloom from December through March, depending on the weather; late January is the most common peak period. The flowers are intensely fragrant and a tree can scent an entire garden, or a single branch an entire house.

Several other trees offer late-winter flowers to brighten the short days of this gray period. Perhaps most common is the white-flowered star magnolia, *Magnolia tomentosa* (formerly *M. stellata)*. It is the earliest blooming of the innumerable magnolias. There are many cultivars of this species, although some hunting may be needed to find them. All are small multistemmed deciduous trees normally eight to ten feet but reaching 20 feet with age. More unusual types include the pink-flowering cultivar *M. tomentosa* 'Rubra' or the many-petaled 'Centennial'. 'Jane Platt' opens to white from pink buds which are large with numerous petals. The Yulan magnolia, *M. denudata*, mentioned earlier is a larger tree reaching 30 to 40 feet. Its flowers have long petals of pure white and are fragrant. A specimen tree in peak bloom is a memorable sight.

The winter-flowering cherry, *Prunus subhirtella* 'Autumnalis', mentioned earlier, is a deciduous tree 20 feet high flowering sporadically with pink blossoms throughout mild winters. With this diffuse flowering it is never quite the knockout of other species which flower all at once. A lesser known, less hardy but incredibly spectacular species of early flowering cherry for winter in zones 8-9 is the Taiwan cherry, *P. campanulata*. It produces masses of showy deep pink to red flowers.

The cornelian cherries, *Cornus mas* and *C. officinalis*, multistemmed deciduous shrubs to small trees in the ten- to 15-foot range, brighten the winter garden with glowing yellow, fragrant clusters of small flowers. People accustomed to dogwoods as trees with large white bracts are always surprised to learn that these vastly different plants are dogwoods. In addition to the flowers which bloom before forsythia, the plants also have attractive flaking bark.

Several additional deciduous shrubs add to the spectrum of winter-flowering plants. Flowering quince, *Chaenomeles speciosa*, has been a favorite of gardeners since the early 1800s. Its showy flowers open whenever there is a spell of a few warm days. There are over 150 cultivars of this three- to eight-foot densely branched shrub. Flower colors range from white through pink, orange and brilliant scarlet. Among some of the best and most available cultivars are: 'Cameo' and 'Toyo-Nishiki' with white, pink and scarlet flowers on the same plant.

Winter honeysuckle ("Breath-of-spring" in colloquial usage), *Lonicera fragrantissima,* is a common, large shrub to ten feet in diameter which bears small, fragrant white flowers throughout winter on warm days. Though rarely as spectacular in bloom as forsythia, its delicate lacy appearance and fragrance make it a favorite. Older plants can be limbed up to make small trees.

Equally familiar and widely planted is the aptly named winter jasmine, *Jasminum nudiflorum,* a smaller shrub with arching branches which reaches four feet in height. It is also an excellent plant for the top of a retaining wall where branches can cascade in a curtain of flowers. The flowers are bright yellow and can appear anytime during the winter after a few warm days.

Another longtime favorite which can bloom at any time of the winter with the proper weather is fragrant wintersweet, *Chimonanthus praecox.* This native of China forms an eight- to 12-foot shrub to small tree, producing starlike waxy flowers which are translucent yellow and sweetly fragrant. The one-inch flowers are rarely profuse enough to make a dramatic impact,

Among the many new cultivars of *Pieris japonica* are ones with red or pink winter flower buds.

but when backlit on a bright winter day their distinctive character makes up for what they lack in mass. Very fragrant, it is a favorite shrub to cut for winter forcing.

Various species of willows are often grown for their unusual showy catkins called pussy willows. The most commonly grown species is *Salix caprea,* but there are also several cultivars worth seeking out. *S. caprea* 'Pendula' is a weeping form of the common pussy willow which is often grafted high on a standard to form a cascading plant of great beauty when in bloom. *S. gracilistyla,* the rosegold pussy

Skimmia japonica's evergreen leaves and clusters of flower buds are attractive through the winter.

The quince's showy flowers open during warm spells.

Several cultivars of the pussy willow are now available.

willow, is a smaller than normal pussy willow reaching five to seven feet in height. It has large catkins which appear relatively early, often flowering by Valentine's Day in this area. A newer species coming into the nursery trade is *S. chaenomeloides* from Japan. Not only are the very large catkins useful for winter interest, but the large, shiny, bright red winter buds make a stunning show after the leaves drop in the fall.

Least common of deciduous winter-flowering shrubs is the February daphne, *Daphne mezereum*, which flowers for four to five weeks in February and March in our

Magnolia tomentosa, star magnolia, is the earliest blooming magnolia.

area. It has showy pale purple fragrant flowers on a plant normally two to four feet in height. Like all daphnes, it can be difficult to establish. Lenten roses, *Helleborus orientalis,* with their white flowers and evergreen foliage, combine well with the leafless stems and purple flowers of the daphne.

Three broad-leaved evergreen shrubs can be added to this list. An evergreen daphne from China, *D. odora,* the fragrant or winter daphne, is an exquisite small shrub two to three feet high with glossy green leaves (or variegated white in one selection) and small, intensely fragrant flowers in shades of white and purple. It is difficult to establish, but worth any effort to do so.

Camellias are extremely common in the South. The two autumn-flowering species, *Camellia sasanqua* and *C. oleifera,* can bloom into mid-December, and the spring-flowering species, *C. japonica,* can begin blooming in late February to March. These classic southern plants form handsome specimens six to 15 feet in height. The three- to four-inch flowers are single or double, white through pink, lavender and bright red. *C. oleifera,* a single, white-flowered species, is the least common of this group. It is the hardiest camellia and can be grown as far north as zone 6. This species can easily tolerate short periods of -10 degree F.

There is a wide range of mahonia species and cultivars, but few are commercially produced. *Mahonia aquifolium* and *M. bealei* are the two most familiar. A series of rare hybrids are outstanding for their winter interest with spectacular December to January flowers in large terminal racemes of bright yellow, fragrant flowers. The American hybrid is *M.* x 'Arthur Menzies', a cross of *M. bealei* x *M. lomarifolia;* English hybrids resulting from *M. japonica* x *M. lomarifolia* crosses include 'Buckland', 'Charity', 'Faith',

'Hope', 'Lionel Fortescue' and 'Winter Sun'. They are spectacular, some reaching 12 feet in height with two-foot inflorescences in mid-winter. All of them are very difficult to find, but I hope nurseries will continue to expand production as they are among the very best ornamental plants.

One rare native evergreen vine will complete this list, which could go on and on. Carolina jessamine, *Gelsemium sempervirens,* is widely grown in the South for its sheets of bright yellow fragrant flowers which appear from February to April, depending on location and weather. The rarer species, *G. rankinii,* swamp jessamine, blooms heavily in November, then sporadically through the winter with another peak in March. It can be grown on trellises, or allowed to ramble through shrubs and into trees, or without support can become a ground cover mat. Although the flowers are yellow like the Carolina jessamine, the swamp jessamine is not fragrant.

The winter-flowering woody plants appear much less commonly than other plants in our gardens because many people don't know about them. When *Prunus mume* or *Hamamelis* bloom in mid-January in an arboretum or garden center, few people are there to get excited about them and purchase them.

Many winter-blooming plants may be less interesting later in the spring season by comparison with the blaze of forsythias, cherries, azaleas and Bradford pears. Most retailers find the plants difficult to sell and instead stock the plants people want to buy. Consequently, wholesale growers find less demand for these relative unknowns and eventually shift their efforts to more marketable plants. Thankfully, there are specialist nurseries across the country who grow these gems of the winter garden. They can be found with some dedicated hunting.

BARNARD'S INN FARM:

A WINTER WALK

ON MARTHA'S VINEYARD

BY POLLY HILL

My garden at Barnard's Inn Farm on Martha's Vineyard lies in deep repose. It breathes softly, imperceptibly. The shimmering flowers of summer, the riotous leaves of autumn are gone. What remains are the strong, enduring, sheltering and quiet forms of trunks and branches.

To walk in the winter garden is to make some discoveries: the elements of design, the contrasting shapes and textures and the silhouettes of deciduous trees, bare of leaves but still familiar. The bald cypress,

POLLY HILL *started an arboretum from seed in 1957 at her Barnard's Inn Farm on Martha's Vineyard in North Tisbury, Massachusetts. Since then she has grown and evaluated thousands of plants, selecting those that are hardy for Zones 5 and 6. Her work has led to the introduction of more than 60 ornamentals including her numerous selections of* Rhododendron *and* Ilex verticillata *'Earlibright' and 'Tiasquam'.*

Taxodium distichum, shows its finely divided, orderly branching. The tulip tree, *Liriodendron tulipifera*, stands tall, its heavy branches turned up at the ends in characteristic fashion. Against a background of pines, bare reaching branches promise a season still to come.

At Barnard's Inn Farm stone walls built 100 or more years ago, when sheep were grazing the land, outline rectangular fields. On Martha's Vineyard the ocean environment shrouds the island in mist, fog or damp to the extent that the individual rocks in the lacy walls ("glacial pebbles," I am told) are greenish, yellowish or dull orange with lichens. In winter the lichens brighten and soften the surface of the walls. The stone walls provide a dominant architectural element that feels indigenous.

I have followed three design principles since beginning an arboretum from seed in l958: Keep the centers of the field open, keep the walls clear of weeds and keep the plantings simple. For 300 years this old sheep farm was gradually carved from the woodland where Indians had roamed. The homestead dates back to 1690. The scale of my garden is human. Rectangular fields on a level turf, enclosed by stone walls, provide a basic ground plan. I have planted about 20 acres surrounded by woods.

The West Field covers about five acres. Within it is a fenced area 300 feet by 35 feet which my husband christened the "Play-Pen." It is surrounded by a ten-foot fence to keep out deer. A conifer collection, planted outside the Play-Pen on the North, provides shelter from wind.

The North Field, about four acres, includes a pine grove, whose center shelters a bower — a partially secluded resting spot. Crabapples and viburnums are featured on the east and west sides of the field. A wildflower garden and lilac collection are planted near the large sheep barn.

Two smaller fields, the Vegetable Field and the Nursery Field, enclose a grove of stewartias, a rose bed, a caged blueberry planting and a pleached hornbeam arbor.

Sites have evolved over the years for large trees, a kousa dogwood allee, several borders and island plantings. They were not created all at one time. Growing my plants from seed allowed me several years to watch them in the nursery and decide on their niche in the garden.

Two large groups provide immediate visual impact in the winter: the conifers and the hollies. In winter the color green is the center of interest in the garden. All else is gray — tan-gray, black-gray or mixed tints of gray. The shingles on the buildings are dark gray, nearly black, from salt air; the grays of the walls, woods, deciduous trees and turf underfoot, all blend together in the winter

A view of the "Play-Pen," surrounded by a ten-foot fence to keep out the deer. A conifer collection planted on the north side provides shelter from the wind.

scene, and so the eye is drawn to green.

The list of the species of conifers that I have found to grow well on the island, after 20 to 30 years' trial, is a long one. What follows is a description of some of my favorites. The incense cedar, *Calocedrus decurrens,* I grew from Longwood Gardens seed. This massive, handsome tree, with splendid bark, is an eye-catcher in winter. Dark green, it is sturdy and thickly twigged. Not all young seedlings survived transplanting, but that is the beauty of a seed program. The plants that remain after 20 to 30 years are those that adapted to their environment.

Another winner is the Nordmann fir, *Abies nordmanniana,* a handsome tall tree with elegant branching and fat-needled twigs. The lower branches sweep the ground. It has grown well, resisting the winds with grace and health.

When leaves fall from the stewartias, above and top, their mottled, many-colored bark is revealed.

57

The Japanese umbrella pine, *Sciadopitys verticillata,* is a plant of unusual distinction. The multiple whorls of shiny leaves, each gracefully curled, are smooth and agreeable to feel. This species succeeds handsomely in many island gardens, achieving far better forms than specimens on the mainland. It is slow when young, but so very worth waiting for.

Abies procera glauca, the blue form of the noble giant fir, is a native of our West Coast. This tree is indeed arresting. The whitish-blue color is its most conspicuous feature. The large, fat cones, which appear on relatively young trees, are 6 to 10 inches long and three to three and a half inches wide, and so erect in the upper branches that they suggest owls overlooking the fields. Their fresh fragrance tempts squirrels to chew or break them up, but the cones are difficult to dislodge and most survive. This fir has potential for enormous height. We shall see.

For many years, as Delawareans, my husband and I have loved the tall stands of loblollies, *Pinus taeda,* on the wide open fields of Sussex County on the Delmarva peninsula. At Barnard's Inn Farm ours were volunteers only inches tall that we moved from the sandy roadsides. Only a dozen survived. Now about thirty years old, their tall bare stems and graceful crowns give filtered light to ericaceous and other understory plants. Only a few have succumbed to the bark beetles that decimated the Japanese black pine, *Pinus thunbergiana,* and the Japanese red pine, *Pinus resinosa,* on the island.

The native white pine *Pinus strobus*

---

*Fossil pollens suggest that both *Pinus taeda* and *P. strobus* were growing here before the last glaciation. Barnard's Inn Farm lies directly below the terminal moraine.

grows well if inland from the salt winds, but none have proved immune to salt burning where exposed. *

Two little-known pines also appear suitable in our environment: *Pinus lambertiana,* western sugar pine, and *Pinus strobiformis.* In youth they are lovely, exceptionally soft and thickly branched. They are still immature. Krussman lists *P. strobiformis* for zone 9, as it comes from Mexico and border states, but it appears quite content thus far in my zone 6 garden.

Among Japanese conifers three more are high on the list of desirables. Japanese white pine, *Pinus parviflora,* an evolving species, is variable and especially beautiful in its cultivated forms which the Japanese refer to as *Pinus pentaphylla.* The Korean pine, *Pinus koraiensis,* with longer needles and large sticky cones bearing edible nuts, is a good staple pine here. The third is *Cryptomeria japonica,* including its many forms. The tall cultivar, 'Yoshino', from the National Arboretum, is splendid. Like *Sciadopitys,* all the cryptomerias do better here than on many mainland sites.

Among the spruces my favorite is *Picea orientalis.* The very short needles are closely set and the whole tree is a rich dark green. The habit is orderly. For entertainment I grow *Araucaria araucana,* the monkey puzzle tree, from Chile and Argentina. It is hardy but slow and always brings a smile for its bizarre silhouette. *Chamaecyparis thyoides,* a native of wet lowlands, is surprisingly carefree and easy to grow in dry, windy, fully exposed sites in my open fields. A thickly fruited individual should be selected for the beauty of its greenish white cones, and planted in more diverse situations. Tall, narrow, pest free and undemanding, the eastern white cedar is a unappreciated native tree.

This listing of my favorite conifers is a

sample of the many species from around the globe that ornament my winter garden. In addition there is one fir tree that I hope to introduce. The seed was given to me in 1959 as *Abies numidica*, but it appears to be instead *Abies lasiocarpa*, now about fifteen feet tall. Narrowly conical in shape, undemanding of space, it has rare distinction. How can I describe a tree whose form seems perfect to its many admirers? It is bluish green, disease free and adds special elegance to the winter garden.

By using the dwarfs and smaller forms of these and other conifers, we have created areas near a bench, inviting us to rest, look around and enjoy the wider view over the fields.

Not all the most conspicuous plants in my winter garden are conifers. There are also hollies, *Ilex*. Sunlight bounces off their leaves. The surface texture of conifers might be compared to fur. If so, then the surface texture of evergreen hollies suggests satin. These are *I. aquifolium,* our southern *I. cornuta* and the glossiest of the *I. opaca.* To easterners *Ilex opaca* is the Christmas holly. It is found wild from eastern Massachusetts to Arizona and Texas.

Native hollies on Martha's Vineyard are handsomely represented by the deciduous holly, *Ilex verticillata,* which is rapidly becoming popular. Locally it is called black alder or winterberry. The best easily available cultivar is 'Winter Red'. An outstanding hybrid from the National Arboretum is 'Sparkleberry'. A dwarf treasure is 'Rock Garden', bred by Elwin Orton at Rutgers University in New Jersey.

There is a group of seven wild cultivars selected and introduced by Barnard's Inn Farm. They differ in such ways as in early or late fruiting; in the colors of their berries, crimson, red or orange; in the size of their fruits and in their plant height. The Vineyard strain has proved to be tough, exceptionally drought tolerant and highly stoloniferous. Their names are 'Bright Horizon', 'Earlibright', 'Tiasquam', 'Quitsa', 'Aquinnah', 'Short Cake' and the male 'Quansoo'.

Among the *Ilex opaca* selections I have named 'Martha's Vineyard' and 'Barnard Luce', both red-fruited females, 'Villanova', with yellow berries, and 'Nelson West', a narrow-leafed male. I also named 'Muffin', a dwarf male *Ilex crenata*, densely twiggy and hardy, from Japanese seed.

Another favorite is the long-stalked holly, *Ilex pedunculosa*, which makes a fine ornamental shrub or small tree during any season. *Ilex aquifolium*, the queen of them all, is on the edge of hardiness here. Nonetheless, 20-foot-high *I. aquifolium* males and females are flourishing. Among them are cultivars 'Ciliata Major', 'Camelliifolia', 'Evangeline' and some unnamed seedlings of my own, which are proving to be attractive survivors.

In my winter garden there are also camellias, rhododendrons and mountain laurels in various shades of green that grow in the borders and islands, that edge the walks and accent the vistas. Because my garden is Zone 6, there is a limit to the broadleafed plants I can grow because of winter winds, cold or drought. The only truly hardy camellia is *Camellia oleifera* from China. It bears beautiful white blooms in October and November. A very few *C. japonica* and their hybrids survive, but are loath to produce flower buds in the average season. Those that do survive bloom in April. Their foliage is astonishingly thick and glossy. I remember that in Japan they grow on the edge of the sea and can be washed with salt spray.

I have also made a special effort to grow

POLLY HILL

A close look at the Nakaharae hybrid azalea 'Alexander'
reveals a red-maroon color on the petioles,
pointed flower buds and the occasional leaf in winter.

every species of tree or shrub known to attract birds. Winter birds clean up the crabapple fruits and shiny silver berries of the local red cedar, *Juniperus virginiana.*

When the earliest witch-hazel, *Hamamelis vernalis,* comes into bloom, waiting insects appear, attracted by the fragrant flowers, and the pollen. Chipmunks and rabbits come out of hiding when *Daphne mezereum* is bursting its buds.

Fragrant *Daphne genkwa,* from Korean seed, as beautiful as any orchid, is a late-winter bloomer, begging for a visit from color-hungry gardeners. The tiniest of daffodils, *Narcissus asturiensis* lifts its two inches through the snow even before the snowdrops are in bloom. *Cyclamen coum* can open its flowers in February and hold on until April, seeking what warmth it can find on clear days. Among early bloomers are the precocious magnolias, whose flowers open before the leaves are fully developed. In winter magnolia flower buds are wrapped in furry coats. All winter these fuzzy gray

points on the the end of every magnolia twig enrich the garden scene.

When leaves fall from the stewartia trees, their mottled, many-colored, bark is revealed. The bark of the paperbark maple peels off in rough brown curls. Small leaves of some rhododendrons contrast with big shiny leaves of others. *Rhododendron yakusimanum* 'Wild Wealth' holds a bald and glistening sphere, the size of a big marble, within a circle of leaves. This is the winter flower bud, formed in August.

Half hidden among the foliage of one of my groundcover azaleas, *Rhododendron* 'Louisa', is a witch's broom, a minutely dainty detail in an already fine-leafed plant. What mite chanced to feed there to make me such a gift? Or what fungus initiated this abnormality?

A close look at the the Nakaharae hybrid azalea 'Alexander' reveals that only in winter does a variable red-maroon color appear on the petioles and the pointed flower buds, and then splash a leaf here and there. When

In winter, ocean mists brighten green, yellow and orange lichens on the old
stone walls which provide a dominant architectural element.
The shrub at center is *Corylopsis sinensis*.

winter sunlight slants at a deep angle into the garden, new shadows make new moods and patterns in once familiar places.

It is good to relax and reflect, once back in the warm house, that the garden is safe for now, at rest, restoring its energies. ✳

The strong, enduring, quiet forms of trunks and branches form a backdrop for
the red fruits of the deciduous native holly, *Ilex verticillata*.

THE WINTER GARDEN
AT THE
SCOTT ARBORETUM

BY CLAIRE SAWYERS

Most of us tend to recognize three seasons in our planting schemes; rarely do we dream about winter gardens or plan and design gardens with that season in mind. To make home gardeners aware of plants that peak in the winter and to recognize the diversity of plants that provide solace during the dormant season, the Scott Arboretum has added a "Winter Garden" to the campus of Swarthmore College, which comprises the Arboretum.

The impetus for this garden was the construction of the college's $14 million Lang Performing Arts Center (PAC). This contemporary structure, completed in 1991, would be most heavily visited by students and the community during the winter

CLAIRE SAWYERS *is the Director of the Scott Arboretum of Swarthmore College. She guest edited two handbooks:* Gardening with Wildflowers and Native Plants *and* Japanese Gardens. *Her articles have also appeared in* Horticulture *and* Fine Gardening.

months. The Arboretum staff wanted to make sure that while exciting performances were being staged inside, visitors would be greeted with an exciting outdoor performance.

While the planting around the PAC is larger than many home gardens, the ideas used here are applicable to suburban and urban gardens. For example, while winter concert goers to the PAC may not brave the January chill to explore the Arboretum, they will enjoy the winter beauty of plants in this specially designed garden by attending some special event. The lesson here is to use plants with winter interest near doorways, entry walkways, driveways and garages since during winter our outdoor activities tend to be restricted to these areas.

Through the Performing Arts Center's window walls visitors inside the lobby notice bright stems, waving clumps of ornamental grasses and a diversity of evergreen leaf textures. The huge windows provide and ornament the lobby like dramatic paintings. Even if you don't have windows of this scale, the relationship between this building and garden illustrates the importance of reserving the vistas through your windows for plants that will inspire you throughout the cold months.

Plants that peak in this winter garden include trees, shrubs and perennials: *Acer palmatum* 'Sango Kaku', which when naked of leaves shows bright orange branches (living up to its common name of coral-bark maple), and *Salix alba* 'Snake' whose unusual fasciated (abnormally flattened and coalesced) growth is apparent once it sheds its leaves and whose pussies' silver hairs glow when back-lit by the late winter sun, and masses of witch-hazels. The Chinese witch-hazel, *Hamamelis mollis*, unrolls yellow petals on warm days beginning in February. The petals roll up again on cold days like party noisemakers. One of the Chinese witch-hazels, *H. mollis* 'Early Bright', a particularly early bloomer in the Winter Garden, is a selection named and introduced by the Scott Arboretum. *Cornus mas* should also be mentioned, for its clusters of pale yellow flowers outline the branches and give a halo effect in late winter.

There are winter-blooming shrubs in the Winter Garden as well, such as *Viburnum* x *bodnantense* 'Dawn' whose pink fragrant flowers brave the first warm winter days and *Jasminum nudiflorum* whose green low-arching stems cascade over walls and bring bright yellow flowers to the garden in late February or early March. *Sarcococca hookeriana* var. *humilis*, a low shrub used in mass as a ground cover, blooms in late winter too. Its tiny flowers would go unnoticed, nestled along the stems under the evergreen leaves, if it weren't for their sweet, powerful fragrance that pervades the air in late February and early March. *Ilex verticillata*, the winterberry holly, is another shrub best in winter.

Its summer flowers are insignificant, its foliage unnoteworthy, but in the fall and winter when its stems are laden with numerous bright red berries, it's a spectacle. There are a number of good cultivars of winterberry holly and several have been used in the Winter Garden.

In the shade of the building, beneath the trees and shrubs, hellebores send up white and rose colored pinwheellike flowers in late winter. Nearby, *Heuchera americana* 'Dale's Strain' covers patches of ground with evergreen leaves mottled with white that have colored garnet in the winter. Here too are the big burgundy winter leaves of bergenias, *Bergenia cordifolia* 'Evening Glow'.

A variety of other plants found in this garden can't be said to peak in the winter but do offer substanial interest, and they provide a bonus of bloom during the growing season. *Crataegus viridis* 'Winter King', a tough hawthorn, has silvery branches with flaky mottled bark in winter, laden with bright red berries, followed by a cloud of white blossoms in the spring. Several cherries in this garden have satiny smooth orangish bark that is hard to resist touching and is of interest year-round: *Prunus* 'Okame', *P. serrula* and *P. subhirtella* 'Autumnalis', the autumn-flowering cherry. These cherries all contribute showy, pale pink blossoms in other seasons.

In the winter the oakleaf hydrangea, *Hydrangea quercifolia*, exhibits flaky-barked stems topped with brown papery flower heads that have persisted from the summer. If the old flowers are left, they last to greet the next batch of fresh white flowers. In addition, the bold leaves of this shrub develop maroon hues in the fall, if grown in sunny situations. This hydrangea should really be regarded as a four-season shrub.

The clusters of pale-yellow flowers of *Cornus mas*, Cornelian cherry, outline the branches in late winter and create a halo effect.

Viburnum dilatatum 'Erie' produces big clusters of plump red berries in the fall. As they persist through the winter, they shrivel but hold their color and remain attractive. Flat clusters of white flowers cover the shrub in the spring and so this plant has two strong seasons of interest.

At ground level *Geranium macrorrhizum* 'Spessart' and *G. cantabrigense* are being counted on for their persistent leaves that sporadically turn wine colored during the winter, but these geraniums are perhaps most vibrant when their flowers are open during the summer.

A variety of trees — pines, evergreen hollies and cedars — and a mix of groundcovers — Christmas ferns, (*Polystichum acrostichoides*), *Cotoneaster salicifolius* 'Scarlet Leader', wild ginger, (*Asarum europaeum*), *Pachysandra procumbens*, *Euonymus fortunei* 'Longwood' and *Liriope muscari* 'White Monroe' have been included in the garden for their evergreen leaves. These plants provide a variety of shapes, forms and textures throughout the year.

As the Winter Garden illustrates, there are many plants to choose from in creating winter wonderlands. Over 75 kinds of plants were selected for this garden and the list of plants we'd like to add keeps growing. Our gardens needn't be devoid of winter interest and gardeners needn't give up on this season. ❊

A SOUTHERN WINTER GARDEN

BY FELDER RUSHING

Camellia sasanqua, one of the most spectacular bloomers in the South's two-month winter season.

I n *A Southern Garden*, Elizabeth Lawrence, perhaps the most thorough gardener to write of her beloved region's gardens, describes in detail the many woody and herbaceous plants of our "two months of winter." She strikes a

FELDER RUSHING *is a horticulturist and seventh generation Mississippi gardener, author and photographer. His small cottage garden is packed with over 300 species of native plants and other popular hardy flowers rescued from Southern gardens.*

tender chord in noting that "We do not have to wait for spring... After the slimy stalks of fall flowers have been cleared away...winter flowers begin to bloom."

Southern gardeners have plenty of chores to do in the winter, just raking leaves and mowing so-called "weeds" in the lawn. Cooking out, taking walks and gardening are popular pastimes, diversions from our bone-deep knowledge that, with little more than overnight notice, weeks of beautiful weather can and will turn chilly, wet, overcast and generally nasty for days on end.

Still, we have more winter vegetable gardens on average than the rest of the nation — we can eat from our gardens nearly all winter long. And we delight in tending oversize containers of shrubs, flowers and herbs through fair weather and foul. Through most of the winter greenhouses are harder to cool than heat; those of us who tend lots of potted tropical plants risk backaches from trotting them in and out of the house during fickle changes in weather.

Caught between the subtropics and more classic temperate zones, Southerners have had to fight for favorite landscape plants. Cold-hardy scattered remnants of ice ages past can be found in the South, left eons ago by glaciers pushing down from Canada. Yet growing side-by-side with tropical escapees from cultivated gardens, many suffer routinely from cold damage — even when the temperatures only hit the mid-teens.

It's not that the temperatures go all that low; they don't. All winter long there are weeks of warm days and moist soils, and it's not unusual to have flowering trees, shrubs, bulbs and other perennials in full bloom any day of the season. In such a relatively mild climate, it's easy to understand how an overnight drop of fifty degrees to even a very light freeze, after days on end of balmy, sunny weather, can wreak havoc in too-tender, sap-risen landscapes.

We've had to learn on our own which plants can take the pendular temperature and moisture effects. For example, an inquiry to the American Peony Society (Hopkins, Minnesota) for tips on those highly prized plants was answered with a curt "Sorry — peonies don't grow in the South." which simply isn't true. Generations of Southern gardeners have found, through trial and error, that the early-blooming peonies are most likely to set bud in low-chilling areas and flower before spring temperatures cause buds to blast. 'Festiva Maxima,' a peony introduced in the 1860s, blooms easily and is passed around by all sorts of gardeners throughout the South.

A leisurely drive through small communities, especially in older neighborhoods and poor parts of town, can turn up some surprising finds. Wintertime, a season of landscape "bones," brings out the best examples of hardy shrubs and tough perennials. Looking past all the store-bought pansies and ornamental kale, an observant gardener will quickly notice such bulbs as oxalis, summer snowflake, *Leucojum* sp., and a double handful of multiplying daffodils, all blooming with little or no help even around abandoned homesites and in old cemeteries. Also common are naturalized masses of two daffodil species in particular, the reedlike jonquil, *Narcissus jonquilla* and multiple-flowered paperwhites, *Narcissus tazetta*, both with heady fragrance. Other aromas fill the air, from the shrubby star magnolia, sweet olive, winter honeysuckle and *Eleagnus*. Other shrubs having mid-winter blooms include *Camellia japonica, C. sasanqua,* spirea, forsythia, quince and mahonia. Bright berries are in abundance on hollies (especially notable are the native deciduous hollies), pyracantha and the ever-popular nandina — that is, until flocks of cedar waxwings devour every berry.

Birdwatching is a popular winter pastime, with many permanent residents and migratory northern species wintering in the South. Their songs, along with the antics of ever-active squirrels, provide a slice of life many gardeners appreciate. We regret the temporary loss of ruby-throated hummingbirds and purple martins in early winter and leave feeders and gourd houses up for their February return. Macabre "trees" of round, brown gourds erected as martin houses stand starkly against the winter sky across the South.

Broadleaf evergreen shrubs serve as mainstays of most landscapes. They provide not only the interesting contrasts of texture and form so important to a winter landscape, but also a surprising amount of variation in hue and shade of green. Depending on the cultivar, the foliage of azaleas alone ranges from light to dark green to burgundy. Hollies are used extensively for their many forms, including generic "gumdrops" such as the dwarf Chinese and yaupon, to tree-form Burford and Foster hybrids and tall American hollies. Professional landscapers and cottage gardeners alike use a great many yuccas, especially the clump-forming, softer forms, *Yucca filamentosa,* along with *Nandina*, for winter texture. Two heavily-favored vines for late winter flowers, Carolina jessamine and coral honeysuckle, *Lonicera sempervirens*, are Southeast natives.

In addition to the overused pampas grass (hardy only in the middle and lower South), other ornamental grasses, including the trendy *Miscanthus* species, can be spotted in many old gardens and even cemeteries, standing out more in winter than in summer. The question of "to prune or not to prune" the old growth in the winter is a common source of argument in many households. North Carolina's Edith Eddleman pitches the idea of simply enjoying the winter effect, or, when it turns taupe after a freeze, spray-painting it in pastels, (unusual, but an enjoyable tweak against stuffiness).

Such widely-used ground covers as liriope, mondo grass, English ivy, *Vinca major*, ajuga and Asiatic jasmine are also making strong inroads into contemporary gardens, as low-maintenance alternatives to turfgrass and for their yin/yang winter contrast with dormant turf and mulches. They really stand out in winter and reduce lawn chores.

It's easy to tell who uses chemical weed killers on southern lawns. The most popular turfgrasses are "warm season" perennial grasses such as St. Augustine, Bermuda, centipede and zoysia. By midwinter, these turfgrasses are dormant, or nearly so. Their browned-out impact is dramatic, prompting visiting English gardeners to wonder if everthing is dead. However, there are many overwintering annual and perennial "weeds" which, left alone, will appear like beacons in well tended lawns.

Most lie low from October until February, but grow rampantly in their late winter flowering phases. Dandelion, henbit, onion and garlic, clovers, *Ranunculus,* spring beauty and even seedling daffodils can quickly turn a lawn into a winter and spring wildflower meadow. This isn't necessarily a bad development, since most are controlled (if desired) simply by mowing in the early spring. They'll be back.

One of my earliest garden thrills was the realization that I was beginning to distinguish different bulbs and perennials by their winter foliage alone. "Gone down" at first frost are the hostas and most ferns, but *Aspidistra* and holly fern, *Cyrtomium falcatum*, remain evergreen in shaded gardens, along with an occasional clump of butcher's broom, *Ruscus,* or nippon lily, *Rhodea. Iris albicans,* or white flag, blooms are seen in nearly every neighborhood across the south, and woodland floors are brightened on frosty mornings with sweet violets, trillium, mayapple and blue phlox,

Phlox divaricata. Other outstanding perennials with winter foliage effects abound: fernlike yarrow, clumps of *Stokesia*, daylilies, *Arum italicum, Lycoris* species, *Artemisia* ('Silver King' is very common) and the always-dependable hellebores. Oddities such as the reedlike *Equisetum*, Spanish moss and hardy bromeliads, are much more noticeable in winter, along with carpets of scaly gray lichens, emerald mosses and shelf fungi on logs, stones and trunks.

Other than the afore-mentioned pansies, kale and dependable Johnny-jump-ups, few winter annuals are bedded out *en masse.* However, a plethora of overwintering biennials and short-lived perennials are set out, including hollyhocks, sweet Williams, lark-spur, fennel, tulips and wildflowers such as coreopsis, queen Anne's lace and gaillardia.

In addition to these widely used landscape plants, garden artwork and hard features give a crucial lift to winter gardens. Human-scale ornaments ranging from fences, birdbaths, sculpture and other hard features fill the need for most gardeners, although a current trend seems to be towards the use of more natural material (boulders, logs, etc.). Compost piles are becoming more acceptable in this era of environmental interest, especially in light of legislation banning leaves and limbs from landfills.

Fellow Southerner Henry Mitchell, in *The Essential Earthman,* asked rhetorically, "What good would a whole orchard full of

A typical Southern lawn chair scene in mid-winter.

ABOVE: A typical Southern winter garden — *Camellia japonica*, smilax vine and nandina.

RIGHT: A ubiquitous gazing ball in February after two weeks of 70°F weather.

daffodils be, if our minds were preoccupied with palm trees?" In a land of six or seven garden seasons a year, which follow one another with little fanfare, the winter garden is only a little less busy than the rest. We may at first have to look harder for color, growth and fragrance, but it's all there. And for those of us who don't pine for other parts of the world, there are sweet rewards.

Southern herb guru Madalene Hill of Texas signs her books with the command "Grow where you are planted." Even in winter, that's saying a lot.   ❄

A WINTER GARDEN IN MINNEAPOLIS

BY THOMAS R. OSLUND

"Nature is full of genius, full of the divinity;
so that not a snowflake escapes its fashioning hand."

Henry David Thoreau

During the long, cold midwest winter, most gardens are abandoned because of their seemingly monochromatic appearance. However, Thoreau's words became my inspiration for a garden that celebrates this magnificent season. In winter the elements of light, shadow, snow and sky may diminish a space, stroke a simple plane or create a sense of solidity. Understanding these elements makes the approach to creating a winter garden one of simple composition.

The Garden

The garden is located in Minneapolis, Minnesota, on a city lot measuring 45 by

THOMAS OSLUND *grew up in Minneapolis and received his MLA at Harvard University. He is currently Vice President and Director of Landscape Architecture In Minneapolis.*

150 feet that slopes upward some 30 feet towards the back of the property. A central axis is created by steps, a walkway leading to the front of the 1920s California bungalow and a crushed stone path leading from the back of the house to the rear property line. Walking up the front steps, one is drawn into the axis through a sloping mass of *Polygonum cuspidatum* var. *compactum*, fleece flower, an invasive groundcover with a wonderful texture and cinnamon winter color that identifies the garden's entrance. The walkway interrupts a hedge ring of *Thuja occidentalis* 'Techny', Techny arborvitae, five feet high that provides color and wind protection at the front entry. Within the hedge ring, *Berberis thunbergii* var. *atropurpurea,* Japanese barberry, and *Euonymus alata*, winged euonymus, recall the windrows of agriculture indigenous to this region. The euonymus, with its corky, horizontal branch

structure, provides a perfect shelf for snow where it elegantly contrasts with vertical foliage of arborvitae. Annual beds, located between hedgerows, allow snow to provide distinctive accent striping.

A straight gravel path continues the axis at the back of the house. A two-level deck terminates at a small reflecting pool and steam fountain. Between the deck and the fountain, a series of simple shapes and textures articulate the remainder of the garden. Framing the deck along its southern edge is a grove of *Phyllostachys aureosulcata,* yellow groove bamboo. The bamboo is intended to be wrapped with white fabric during the winter months for protection and unveiled once the spring arrives.

Along the northern facade of the garage/guest house, a square shaped stand of *Cornus sericea,* red osier dogwood, demarcates the eastern corner of the garden. Their red stems, saturated with strong winter light, provide a spectacular accent against the drifting snow. *Andropogon scoparius,* little bluestem prairie grass, provides the

ground texture for the rest of the garden.

The clump growth habit of this grass makes for an intriguing undulating pattern under a blanket of snow. Located within the prairie grass are the angled raised lawn areas and concentric perennial rings. These two elements are contained by native dryset limestone (Mankato Kasota Stone), selected for its rich golden color, contrast and its ability to reflect and illuminate the intense winter sun.

The one-foot elevated planes of the lawn platform and perennial rings allow snow to "ghost" the garden and long shadows to play off its contours. At the rear of the property, where the land slopes upward, a double row of *Betula nigra,* river birch,

71

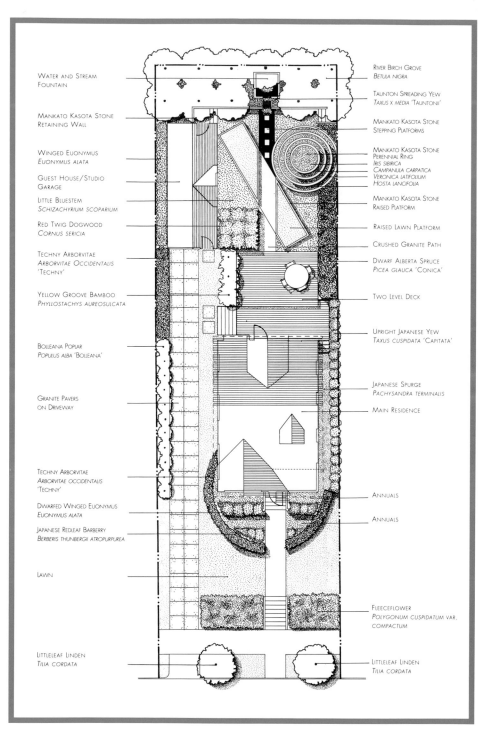

WATER AND STREAM
FOUNTAIN

MANKATO KASOTA STONE
RETAINING WALL

WINGED EUONYMUS
Euonymus alata

GUEST HOUSE/STUDIO
GARAGE

LITTLE BLUESTEM
Schizachyrium scoparium

RED TWIG DOGWOOD
Cornus sericia

TECHNY ARBORVITAE
*Arborvitae Occidentalis
'Techny'*

YELLOW GROOVE BAMBOO
Phyllostachys aureosulcata

BOLLEANA POPLAR
Populus alba 'Bolleana'

GRANITE PAVERS
ON DRIVEWAY

TECHNY ARBORVITAE
*Arborvitae occidentalis
'Techny'*

DWARFED WINGED EUONYMUS
Euonymus alata

JAPANESE REDLEAF BARBERRY
Berberis thunbergii atropurpurea

LAWN

LITTLELEAF LINDEN
Tilia cordata

RIVER BIRCH GROVE
Betula nigra

TAUNTON SPREADING YEW
Taxus x media 'Tauntonii'

MANKATO KASOTA STONE
STEPPING PLATFORMS

MANKATO KASOTA STONE
PERENNIAL RING
*Iris sibirica
Campanula carpatica
Veronica latifolium
Hosta lancifolia*

MANKATO KASOTA STONE
RAISED PLATFORM

RAISED LAWN PLATFORM

CRUSHED GRANITE PATH

DWARF ALBERTA SPRUCE
Picea glauca 'Conica'

TWO LEVEL DECK

UPRIGHT JAPANESE YEW
Taxus cuspidata 'Capitata'

JAPANESE SPURGE
Pachysandra terminalis

MAIN RESIDENCE

ANNUALS

ANNUALS

FLEECEFLOWER
*Polygonum cuspidatum var.
compactum*

LITTLELEAF LINDEN
Tilia cordata

frames the view to the fountain. The tan, peeling birch trunks create an evenly spaced pattern of vertical forms.

Taxus x *media* 'Tauntonii', Taunton spreading yew, provides a contrasting evergreen groundcover beneath the birch grove. In front of the birch grove, a four-foot high limestone dryset stone wall takes up the change in grade. Its rough textured surface provides yet another contrast between the birch and snow. The steam fountain cascades two feet into a cistern pool, spills through the retaining wall, and drops another two feet to a reflecting pool with stepping platforms.

The northern property line is defined by two types of evergreens, *Taxus cuspidata* 'Capitata', upright Japanese yew, and *Picea glauca* 'Conica', dwarf Alberta spruce. These evergreens screen the garden from adjacent properties and help protect it from the prevailing winter winds.

The southern property line is composed of *Populus alba* 'Pyramidalis', Bolleana poplar, *Thuja occidentalis* 'Techny' and *Euonymus alata*. The line of poplars defines the driveway edge and allows the low winter sun to penetrate the rest of the garden, creating intricate shadow patterns across the granite drive.

This winter garden begins to explore the subtle, yet intricate, balance among the elements of shadow, light, snow, stone, steam and plants to bring new life to a place usually perceived to be dormant. Unlike a summer, fall or spring garden, a winter garden gives a sense of life that cannot be achieved simply with the growth and change of plants. One must begin to understand, as Thoreau did, the structure of nature and the inherent qualities and forces acting upon nature. By understanding these intricacies, and artfully composing the garden's elements, one sees the endless possibilities for a winter garden landscape. Not to mention the garden's year-round possibilities. ❄

The clump growth habit of little bluestem makes for an intriguing undulating pattern under a blanket of snow.

A CALIFORNIA GARDEN

IN WINTER

BY MARSHALL OLBRICH

California gardeners, especially those in its coastal areas, share a "Mediterranean climate." This means six months of warm, dry weather, followed by six months of colder rainy weather. Disregarding the drought of the last few years, the amount of annual rainfall in different parts of California varies widely. The southern counties are very dry, San Diego receiving a very few inches; in central California rainfall is more moderate, the Bay Area around San Francisco receiving 22 inches, and in the north, the rain in some places exceeds 100 inches.

My garden is in the coastal redwood area about 60 miles north of San Francisco. On average, we get 60 inches of rain which, compressed into the winter months,

MARSHALL OLBRICH, *a horticulturist and writer, was the owner of Western Hills Rare Plant Nursery in Occidental, California. His articles appeared in* Horticulture *and* Pacific Horticulture.

makes for a high water table and generally soggy soil. Climate extremes are not so much between cold and hot, as between too much water in winter and too little in the summer. The roots of many plants do not grow below the water table, which can be only a foot or two below the surface. The danger is that plants may have roots too shallow and insufficient to withstand the long dry season.

Our temperature range is broader than that in fog-cushioned San Francisco. On the positive side, our additional heat (up past 90 degrees F at times) allows us to flower plants like *Daphne odora* and obtain viable seed on some maples. On the other hand, our low temperatures (with some nights 25 degrees F or lower) rule out subtropicals like *Bougainvillea, Lantana, Heliotrope, Poinsettia, Pelargonium* and other plants commonplace in the Bay Area.

In fall and winter, we share three groups of plants with eastern and midwestern gardeners: hardy perennials, which tend to bloom very late in the year, trees with fall color, and ornamental grasses. Though our trees can't compare in color with eastern forests, we have a few successes. The bald cypress, *Taxodium distichum*, now 30 years old, is very striking with its fox-red deciduous foliage. (This year its "evergreen" Mexican counterpart, the Montezuma cypress, also colored and lost its needles.)

The sweetgum, *Liquidambar styraciflua*, and keaki elm, *Zelkova serrata,* color well, as does the coral-bark variety of Japanese maple, *Acer palmatum* 'Sango Kaku'. Two trees are unusual here in the lateness of color and leaf-drop: The Mexican hawthorn, *Crataegus pubescens*, may be in color as late as February. A striped-bark maple from Taiwan, *Acer morrisonense,* will color and drop its leaves as late as the end of January, with spring growth starting almost immediately, so that by March it is full again.

In general, however, fall color is poor and disappointing. Because of our dry and warm September and October weather, trees famous for their color, like the quaking aspen, the katsura tree *(Cercidiphyllum japonicum) Parrotia persica* and others dry up and drop their leaves with no ceremony at all.

Grasses are as important in winter here as they are in the East, providing accents in otherwise blank areas. We tend to associate them with more tender spiky plants like New Zealand flax, *Phormium tenax* — in the newer, highly colored, varieties — and *Dasylirion* spp., western plants which make symmetrical six-foot mounds of needle sharp foliage. Pampas grass, in its variegated varieties,j grows well, and its New Zealand relative, *Cortaderia richardii,* with lovely one-sided feathery flower heads, is an asset. Large grasses such as the bluish

Mediterranean evergreen *Helictotrichon sempervirens* and *Miscanthus* species are basic to our winter garden.

As December approaches the elegant small-leaved and small-flowered camellias start to bloom. In general, these are smaller shrubs of great beauty and distinction, but sadly of limited availability. With new species being imported, this group is being hybridized for greater hardiness and certainly should be tried in the milder parts of the eastern United States. We also can grow a number of plants, mostly from Mexico, which, frankly, are more tender but very spectacular, blooming in mid-winter. Foremost of these are the tree dahlias, *Dahlia imperialis* and related species, which may reach 20 feet with feeding and watering; and the giant bushy sages, *Salvia* spp., ranging from deep red to rose pinks, to many shades of blue or purple, and to the clear yellow of *Salvia maderensis*. These sages may range from five to 15 feet high.

I wish this were the end of the story. Unfortunately, during December of 1990, we had, along with most of coastal California, the longest and most devastating freeze in 60 years. We had a warning in 1972, when temperatures went down to 14 degrees F for several nights and stayed below the freezing point for two weeks. We had rashly planted West Australian and South African trees and shrubs, little known in cultivation at that time, and so lost a third of our garden.

The recent cold spell was more extreme and prolonged, going down to an unprecedented 10 degrees F for several nights and not rising above the freezing point for weeks. We were no longer growing the West Australian trees and shrubs, but had disastrous damage to others assumed to be hardy here. The showy Mexican dahlias and sages turned into limp, gray ghosts. Among those affected were two shrubs possibly familiar to southeastern gardeners — *Mahonia lomariifolia*, already in full golden bloom, but losing its flowers and new growth, and *Loropetalum chinense*, again in bloom but alive only as a large mound of dead gray leaves.

New Zealand plants suffered the most unexpected damage — Australian tea bush, *Leptospermum scoparium* and its varieties, were killed outright. Since they, along with the red bottlebrushes, were common plants in the coastal redwood area, evidence of their destruction is everywhere. Other New Zealand plants that may be familiar to southeastern gardeners are *Pittosporum* spp., sometimes killed, sometimes unharmed, and the *Veronica* relatives, the *Hebe* spp., again damaged in different degrees. The colorful forms of New Zealand flax, *Phormium* varieties, and the cabbage tree, *Cordyline* spp., may or may not recover.

As I write in late January, we are hoping that with warmer weather we will find new shoots on some plants, but equally fearing that warmth will kill apparently healthy plants whose roots have rotted. Most of the Bay Area gardens and nurseries are in the same predicament.

Although it's hard to think positively at this point, the disaster can be seen as an opportunity to make an essentially new garden. After all, as it has aged over 30 years, the garden has become too shady. So we are casting a cold eye on even prospering trees and shrubs, with the aim of letting in more light and replanting with hardier perennials and shrubs. Doubtless we shall, sooner or later, succumb to plants of borderline hardiness. If our own resilience doesn't melt away, we will have a pleasing garden once again.   ❋

Populus tremuloides, foreground, and the fox-red deciduous foliage of bald cypress, *Taxodium distichum*.

Spectacular flowering sages, top and above, from Central and South America
bloom in midwinter in California but suffered during the
devastating freeze of December 1990.

77

A WINTER GARDEN IN CAMBRIDGE

BY PETER ORRISS

A walk through the Winter Garden at Cambridge on a clear, crisp, winter morning is an exhilarating experience. The color, form and charm cannot be equaled in any other season. Although frost and snow may enhance the scene in the garden during the winter months, they are not necessary here, for the attraction is flower, foliage, fruit or colored bark. Selecting plants and putting them together in a confined area is what garden artistry is all about, but to do this in what is considered by many to be the dormant season is comparatively recent and becoming fashionable.

The climate in Cambridge in many ways is more suitable for winter display than elsewhere, for there are many clear bright days and this enhances the color of stems. The low angle of the sun provides silhouette and contrast of sun and shade. The bright days are often associated with low temperatures, and although there is little protection in East Anglia from the Arctic cold, Cambridge is only 40 feet above sea-level, and sub-zero temperatures are rare

and seldom last long. The wind chill is serious and desiccation of foliage can occur in Cambridge. Rain and snowfall are light — an average of 21 inches of precipitation per year. Irrigation is essential during most summers to encourage strong annual growth. The soil, a thin, impoverished alluvial river bed with a pH of 7.5, is well drained alkaline overlying gravel.

The idea of creating a winter garden at Cambridge was first conceived in 1951 by John Gilmour, then Director of the Cambridge Botanic Garden. Designed as a formal feature within the Botanic Garden, the Winter Garden formed a long, narrow corridor linking the mature half of the Garden dating back to 1846 with an adjoining part of the garden developed since 1951. In the 1970s, out of the need for more research space and the reluctance to dispose of the winter display , the decision was made to relocate the Winter Garden to another area in the Botanic Garden.

An open area of approximately 100 yards by 35 yards was selected to separate the refreshment area and the more scientific areas of the Garden. In an effort to make it a low-maintenance garden, the formal design of the original garden was abandoned and a theme was developed using

PETER ORRISS *is the Superintendent of the University Botanic Garden, Cambridge, England.*

different groundcovers. Those who know Cambridge will know that undulation, however small, is at a premium — the Garden is as flat as the proverbial pancake and as flat as the surrounding Fens of East Anglia. Undulation had to be created and is now the strongest design element of the garden. We are extremely pleased that we went to the expense of creating a shallow depression through the central area of the Winter Garden. Two shallow valleys, facing southwest and southeast (to maximize the angle of the winter sun) were also created to form banks for the low prostrate plants to tumble down and to provide higher points on which to plant flowering shrubs and small trees.

The Winter Garden is protected by *Taxus baccata* on the North side; *Thuja occidentalis* to the West and *Cupressocyparis leylandii* 'Haggerston Gray', leyland cypress, to the East. Because the garden runs East to West, low-growing hedges were planted along the South side, providing an enclosed area with open views (over the tops of the hedges) from a main path outside the Winter Garden. A winding gravel path leads visitors into the Winter Garden.

The framework of the Winter Garden was established with standard trees strategically placed throughout to give focal points and to screen unsightly background objects. Flowering trees in winter are limited to early flowering cherries, *Prunus subhirtella* 'Autumnalis', a must with its profusion of dainty white flowers first appearing in November and continuing into January; a very close second is the form 'Rosea' with pinkish tints. Both are deserving of their prominent positions in the Garden. The two forms of *Prunus davidiana,* 'Alba' and 'Rubra', are free-flowering in January, provided the weather is not too severe, while later *Prunus incisa*

'February Pink' and later still, in March, *Prunus hirtipes* herald the spring-flowering Japanese cherries in other parts of the Garden. *Prunus serrula* with its beautiful, polished mahogany bark is worthy of a place in any winter scheme. The crabapple *Malus* 'Red Sentinel' is by far the most successful fruiting tree we have, the large red fruits persisting well into January.

Additional height and interest can be achieved by the use of trees with attractive barks, and my favorite is *Betula alba sinensis* var. *septentrionalis*, an Asian species with very attractive peeling bark of shiny flesh color. One of the better white-stemmed birches is the one raised at Hilliers Nurseries at Winchester called *Betula* 'Jermyns'. The snow-white peeling bark retains its whiteness for many years. Maples, too, offer one or two species with attractive bark; none more so than *Acer griseum*, the paperbark maple from central China which displays brilliant crimson autumn foliage and whose main trunk and primary branches flake with curls of shaggy, rich, deep, rusty bark. *Acer grosseri*, also from central China; *Acer capillipes* from Japan; and *A. pensylvanica* from North America, are three maples that produce interesting striated or snake barks, prominent in the dormant season.

Lawson's cypress and other conifers provide a diversity of shape and color. The golden yellow form *Chamaecyparis lawsoniana* 'Winston Churchill' is one of the best yellow forms, while 'Pembury Blue' is a good blue-gray.

The flowering shrubs provide not only the intermediate or eye-level layer of the Garden, but also the perfume. It still remains a mystery to me why so many of our favorite winter-flowering shrubs such as *Chimonanthus praecox* , the winter sweet, *Hamamelis,* witch-hazel, *Lonicera sp.*, the winter-flowering honeysuckle, and many of the viburnums have such sweet scented flowers and yet very few insects are about for pollination. Their loss, however, is our gain and one cannot but want to plant as many of these shrubs as space allows. In the late autumn and early winter the sweet scent of viburnums fills the air. The first to flower is *Viburnum farreri*, which flowers in October before autumn leaf fall and continues on and off into February and March, depending on how severe the weather is. A little later, in November, *Viburnum bodnantense* 'Dawn' flowers with its deep pink, scented flowers — a much larger and more vigorous shrub than *V. farreri*.

With the turning of the year, many old favorites begin to show that spring is not too far away: the winter-flowering jasmine, *Jasminum nudiflorum;* the honeysuckles, *Lonicera fragrantissima, L. standishii* and their hybrid *L.* x *purpusii*; the witch-hazels, *Hamamelis mollis, H.* x *intermedia* 'Jelena' with orange flowers and the deep red form 'Diana' , making a complete contrast to the more common yellow-flowering types. One of my favorite plants in the Winter Garden is the pale yellow form of winter sweet, *Chimonanthus praecox* 'Luteus', sometimes known as *C. praecox* 'Concolor'. To me, it is a far superior plant to the type. Well worth the ten year wait, it is finally beginning to flower profusely with little waxy, bell-shaped, scented flowers of lemon yellow.

The most striking impact of the whole Winter Garden is made by the use of colored stems. The young growth of a number of different genera provides color throughout the winter season. During the dull days of early winter nothing shows up quite so well as the white stems of the bramble from the Himalayas, *Rubus biflorus*. The white "bloom" which appears

only on the young growth gradually wears off within the first year. The stems then become a brownish color which, if left, will produce a good crop of orange-colored blackberries. To maintain a good supply of young white stems, these fruiting shoots should be cut down each spring, as soon as young growth starts to appear at the base of the plant. Ideal for brightening a dark

The color, form and charm of the Cambridge winter garden is unequalled in any other season.

corner of the garden, this bramble shows up well against the dark green of a yew hedge — especially on a moonlit night!

Planted in irregular blocks, the bright red stems of *Cornus alba* 'Sibirica' and the contrasting yellow stems of *Cornus stolonifera* 'Flaviramea', make a bold splash of color. The yellow-stemmed form is a more vigorous plant; therefore, to achieve a balance of contrast, more red-stemmed plants are needed. Although the Cambridge garden is relatively dry, the orange-red *Salix alba* var. *chermesina* and the grayish-white of *Salix irrorata* have proven to be the two most exciting and successful willows. *Salix irrorata* has an added bonus of yellowish-orange catkins in the spring. to get the best effect from colored-stemmed plants, they must be pruned back each year in the spring, for it is the long, thin, annual growth that produces the color. Because the red-stemmed *Cornus* are not as vigorous we reduce the crown by half each year rather than cut back to the ground.

To complete the overall picture, the

CAMBRIDGE WINTER GARDEN PLANTS

TREES WITH FLOWERS OR ATTRACTIVE BARK:

Acer capillipes
A. grosseri
A. grosseri var. hersii
Betula albo-sinensis var.
septentrionalis
B. 'Jermyns'
Malus 'Red Sentinel'
Prunus davidiana 'Alba

Prunus davidiana 'Rubra'
P. hirtipes
P. incisa 'February Pink'
P. hirtipes
P. mume 'Alphandii'
P. rufa
P. subhirtella 'Autumnalis Rosea'
Sorbus acuparia 'Rubra'

SHRUBS: FLOWERING/FRUITING:

Arbutus unedo 'Rubra'
Berberis wilsoniae 'Gerdien'
B. wilsoniae 'Marianne'
Chimonanthus praecox
C. praecox var. grandiflorus
C. praecox var. praecox
Colletia armata
C. cruciata
Cornus mas
C. mas 'Variegata'
Cotoneaster horizontalis
C. lacteus
C. microphyllus var. conspicuus
C. salicifolius 'Autumn Fire'
Erica carnea 'Aurea'
E. carnea 'Fox Hollow'
E. carnea 'James Backhouse'
E. carnea 'King George'
E. carnea 'Snow Queen'
E. carnea 'Springwood Pink'
E. carnea 'Vivellii'
E. erigena 'Superba'
E. erigena 'W.T. Rackliff'

Hamamelis japonica
'Zuccariniana'
H. mollis
H. mollis 'Pallida'
H. x intermedia 'Diane'
H. x intermedia 'Jelena'
Ilex x altaclarensis 'J.C. van Tol'
Lonicera fragrantissima
L. setifera
L. standishii
L. x purpusii
Mahonia japonica
M. x media 'Winter Sun'
Stachyrus praecox
Symphoricarpus 'Hancock'
S. 'White Hedge'
Viburnum carlesii
V. farreri
V. foetens
V. tinus
V. tinus 'Lucidum'
V. tinus 'Variegatum'
V. x bodnantense 'Dawn'

ground cover and ground flora were drifted throughout the garden. It is important not to be too formal or regimented when filling in the areas between the principal plants. A natu- ralistic approach with disregard to exact spacing and using groups of irregular sizes and shapes enhances the overall effect. Never plant in a straight line at equal distance!

E. terminalis
E. x darleyensis 'George Rendall'
Forsythia giraldiana

V. x bodnantense 'Deben'
V. x juddii

SHRUBS WITH COLORED STEMS OR GROUND-COVER FOLIAGE:

Berberis dictyophylla
B. wilsoniae 'Gerdien'
B. wilsoniae 'Illse'
B. wilsoniae 'Marianne'
Cornus alba 'Kesselringii'
C. alba 'Sibirica'
C. stolonifera 'Flaviramea'
Euonymus fortunei var.
radicans 'Variegatus'
Hedera colchica 'Dento-variegata'
H. helix 'Buttercup'
H. helix 'Glacier'
H. helix 'Gold Heart'

H. helix 'Little Diamond'
H. helix 'Lutzil
H. helix 'Marmorata'
H. helix 'Meagheri'
H. helix 'Sagittifolia Variegata'
Ilex aquifolium 'Silver Queen'
Mahonia aquifolium 'Atropurea'
Rubus biflorus
R. niveus
Salix alba var. chermesina
S. irrorata
Stranvaesia davidiana

CONIFEROUS PLANTS:

Chamaecyparis lawsoniana 'Kilmacurragh'
C. lawsoniana 'Pembury Blue'
C. lawsoniana 'Winston Churchill'
C. lawsoniana 'Wisselii'
Cryptomeria japonica 'Elegans Compacta'
Cupressus glabra 'Conica'
Juniperus chinensis 'Stricta'
J. virginina 'Burkii'

J. virginina 'Grey Owl'
Taxus baccata 'Fastigiata Aurea'
T. baccata 'Semperaurea'
Thuja occidentalis
'Ellwangerana'
T. occidentalis
'Ericoides'

BULBOUS AND HERBACEOUS PLANTS:

Bergenia cordiflora
Crocus biflorus
C. chrysanthus 'Snow Bunting'
C sieberi var. atticus
Chionodoxa sardensis
Eranthis hyemalis
E. x tubergenii
Galanthus spp.

Helleborus foetidus
H. guttatus
H. lividus spp. corsicus
H. niger
H. orientalis
Hyacinthella azurea
Narcissus jonquilla
Scilla siberica

The lime-tolerant winter-flowering heathers, cultivars of *Erica carnea* and *Erica* x *darleyensis,* were used predominantly in the more open spaces. Although there are a considerable number of named varieties of heather, they only appear in shades of red, pink and white and there appears to be little to choose among them. *E.* x *daryleyensis* varieties are more vigorous and make slightly larger plants. Ivies of different leaf form make ideal ground covers at this time of year and also provide summer interest. The large creamy-green variegated leaves of *Hedera colchica* 'Dentato-Variegata' give a bold display, while the smaller silver gray leaves of *Hedera helix* 'Glacier' certainly live up to their name on a crisp, frosty morning. We have this plant tumbling down a shallow bank in a serpentine band, looking like a minature glacier.

Euonymus fortunei 'Silver Queen', with its interesting leaf variegation of cream tinged with purple on a dark-green background, makes an ideal groundcover for winter effect and, interplanted with the red stemmed *Cornus,* is a combination well worth repeating. Some of the best combinations are the result of planting bulbs or corms with shrubs or herbaceous plants. I particularly like the combination of *Scilla sibirica* under the early-flowering *Forsythia giraldiana;* blue and yellow make a delightful picture.

There is no doubt that if climate and soil are conducive, plants in winter can give a long lasting display. With careful selection of plants for form, texture and variegation, a winter garden can be attractive from October into April. In the Cambridge University Botanic Winter Garden many people have the opportunity to see and enjoy these plants during an otherwise dreary time of year.   ❄

Planted in irregular blocks, the bright red stems of
Cornus alba 'Sibirica' and contrasting yellow stems of *Cornus sericea*
'Flaviramea' provide bold splashes of color.

Conifers provide a diversity of shapes and colors.

Ground covers are planted in naturalistic drifts
throughout the garden.
In bloom at center is winter aconite, *Eranthis hyemalis*.

WINTER GARDEN
SOURCE LIST

The following is a list of selected nurseries which carry hard-to-find plants. (Unfortunately, we don't have the space to list them all.) If you can't find one of the species or cultivars mentioned in this handbook at your favorite nursery, check the sources listed below.

BULBS

DAFFODIL MART
Route 3, Box 794
Gloucester, VA 23061
804-693-3966

McCLURE AND ZIMMERMAN
108 West Winnebago
P.O. Box 368
Friesland, WI 53935
414-326-4220

MONTROSE NURSERY
P.O. Box 957
Hillsborough, NC 27278
919-732-7787

P. AND J. CHRISTIAN
P.O. Box 468
Wrexham, Clwyd
United Kingdom LL13 9XR(0978)
366 399

DECIDUOUS HOLLIES

BULL VALLEY RHODODENDRON NURSERY
214 Bull Valley Road
Aspers, PA 17304
717-677-6313

CARROLL GARDENS
444 East Main St., Box 310
Westminster, MD 21157
301-848-5422

EASTERN PLANT SPECIALTIES
Box 226
Georgetown Island, ME 04548
207-371-2888

GREENBRIER FARMS, INC.
201 Hickory Road West
Chesapeake, VA 23322
804-421-2141

PRINCETON NURSERIES
P.O. Box 191
Princeton, NJ 08542
609-924-1776

ROSLYN NURSERY
211 Burrs Lane
Six Hills, NY 11746
516-643-9347

MAGNOLIA NURSERY
Route 1, Box 87
Chunchula, AL 36521
205-675-4696

HELLEBORES

FORESTFARM
990 Tetherow Road
Williams, OR 97544
503-846-6963

GOSSLER FARMS NURSERY
1200 Weaver Road
Springfield OR 97478
503-746-3922

GREER GARDENS
1280 Goodpasture Island Rd.
Eugene, OR 97401
503-686-8266

MAPLETHORPE
11296 Sunnyview NE
Salem, OR 97301
503-362-5121

SHADY OAKS NURSERY
700 19th Avenue N.E.
Waseca, MN 56093

WINTER SURVIVAL TACTICS

To relieve the winter doldrums, force bulbs indoors.

Have your child assist you in turning the Christmas tree into mulch.

ELVIN MCDONALD

FELDER RUSHING

THOMPSON AND MORGAN
P.O. Box 1308 ,
Jackson, NJ 08527
201-363-2225

ANDRE VIETTE FARM AND NURSERY
Route 1, Box 16
Fishersville, VA 22939
703-943-2315

ELVIN MCDONALD

Use antidesiccant sprays to protect plants in winter.

Liven up the winter garden with a creatively wrapped shrub.

ORNAMENTAL GRASSES

KURT BLUEMEL, INC.
2543 Hess Road
Fallston, MD 21047
301-557-7229

PRAIRIE NURSERY
P.O. Box 365
Westerfield, WI 53964
608-296-3679

SANDY MUSH HERBS
Route 2, Surrett Cove Road
Leicester, NC 28748
704-683-2014

THOMPSON AND MORGAN
Box 1308
Jackson, NJ 08527
201-363-2225

TREES & SHRUBS

CAMELLIA FOREST NURSERY
P.O. Box 291
Chapel Hill, NC 27514
919-967-5529

CARROLL GARDENS
444 East Main Street
Westminster, MD 21157
301-848-5422

FOREST FARM NURSERY
990 Tetherow Road
Williams, OR 97544
503-846-6963

GOSSLER FARMS NURSERY
1200 Weaver Road
Springfield, OR 97477
503-746-3922

GREER GARDENS
1280 Goodpasture Island Rd.
Eugene, OR 97477
503-686-8266

HERONSWOOD NURSERY
7530 288th Street NE
Kingston, WA 98346
206-297-4172

HOLBROOK FARMS NURSERY
Rte. 2, Box 223B
Fletcher, NC 28732
704-891-7790

MONTROSE NURSERY
P.O. Box 957
Hillsborough, NC 27278
919- 732-7787

NICHE GARDENS
111 Dawson Road
Chapel Hill, NC 27516
919-967-0078

POWELL'S GARDENS
Rte. 3, Box 21
Princeton, NC 27569
919-936-4421

ROSLYN NURSERY
211 Burrs Lane
Dix Hills, NY 11746
516-543-9347

SALTER TREE FARM
Rte. 2, Box 1332
Madison, FL 32340
904-973-6312

SPRINGDALE FARM NURSERY
Mozier Hollow Road
Hamburg, IL 62045

WASHINGTON EVERGREEN NURSERY
P.O. Box 388
Brooks Branch Road
Leicester, NC 28748
704-683-4518

WAYSIDE GARDENS
Hodges, SC 29695-0001
800-845-1124

WE-DU NURSERY
Rte. 5, Box 724
Marion, NC 28752
704-738-8300

WOODLANDER'S NURSERY
1128 Colleton Avenue
Aiken, SC 29801
803-648-7522

VIOLA LABORADORICA

CARROLL GARDENS
444 East Main St., Box 310
Westminster, MD 21157
301-848-5422

LAMB NURSERIES
E. 101 Sharp Avenue
Spokane, WA 99202
509-328-7956

Winter's Hips, Fruits & Berries

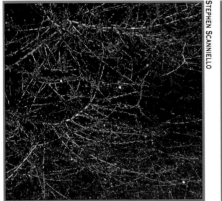

Cottoneaster

Rose hips

Crataegus 'Winter King'

Ilex berries

Malus 'Red Jade'

Lonicera maackii podocarpa

Pyracantha

Viburnum sp.

I N D E X

JOANNE PAVIA

Bulbs add splashes of color to the late winter garden.